# THE GREAT PATRIOT
# PATRIOT
## PROTEST & BOYCOTT BOOK

# THE GREAT PATRIOT

# PATRIOT

## PROTEST & BOYCOTT BOOK

### THE PRICELESS LIST FOR CONSERVATIVES, CHRISTIANS, PATRIOTS, & 80+ MILLION TRUMP WARRIORS TO CANCEL "CANCEL CULTURE" AND SAVE AMERICA!

## WAYNE ALLYN ROOT
### & NICKY BILLOU

Published by Redwood Publishing, LLC
Orange County, California
info@redwooddigitalpublishing.com
www.redwooddigitalpublishing.com

Printed in the United States of America
First Printing, 2021

ISBN 978-1-952106-99-6 (paperback)
ISBN 978-1-7344254-9-9 (ebook)
Library of Congress Control Number: 2021913517

Book Design by Ghislain Viau, Creative Book Design
Cover Design by Graphique Designs, LLC

Disclaimer: All information included in this book is public record and readily available to the general public. Although the author and publisher have made every effort to ensure that the information in this book was correct at press time, the author and publisher do no assume and hereby disclaim any liability to any party for any loss, damage, or disruption caused by errors or omissions, whether such errors or omissions result from negligence, accident, or any other cause.

This book is dedicated to:

God, family, and country.
Personal and economic freedom.
Free Speech.
The 45th President of United States, Donald J. Trump.
And to conservative patriots everywhere.
God bless the USA.

# ACKNOWLEDGMENTS

Special thanks to our publisher, Sara Stratton, and our team of researchers, without which this book could never have happened.

# TABLE OF CONTENTS

# INTRODUCTION

**We Have the Power!**

F olks, this is perhaps the simplest book ever written. It's simply a compilation of the emails, physical mailing addresses, phone numbers and executive leadership (CEO, Chairman of Board, etc) of the 100+ leading corporations in America which are treating conservatives, Christians and patriots like dirt.

We (conservatives, Christians, patriots, Trump deplorables) make up at least half of their customers, more likely 60% or more (because of course, conservatives are the middle class, upper middle class and most business owners—so we spend a majority of the money). Yet these companies, CEOs and their Board have decided to slander us, hate us, offend us and screw us.

**It's time to fight back!**

Liberals (i.e. assorted socialists, Marxists, communists and America-haters) are great at this.

So are civil rights leaders (think Jesse Jackson, Al Sharpton, and BLM) and gay rights leaders.

They aren't afraid to make their voices heard, or their opinions known. And I respect that.

It's time we listened, learned and copied the left's hardball tactics. This book will allow 74 million Trump voters to "model" Jesse Jackson, Al Sharpton, and BLM. Isn't irony delicious?

For far too long, we (the Silent Majority) have been far too silent. I guess that's where we got the name. But we can't afford to be silent any longer. The future of our country, our lives, our careers, our children's lives, are all on the line. We are inches from the end of America.

We have the real power, but we've been too busy working, and raising our families, and paying our taxes, and going to church, or too polite, to use our power.

That has to change TODAY!

It's time to understand we hold the power with our tremendous disposable income and buying power. We aren't going to be silent anymore. We can't be. Or the greatest country in world history, ever blessed by God, will be destroyed and gone forever.

We aren't just the "Silent Majority." We are the spending majority too! Did you know that senior citizens in the United States have a net worth of more than $1.6 TRILLION? AND a majority of seniors are invested in the stock market, with an average investment of $100,000!

Americans over 60 possess tremendous wealth and therefore we can wield tremendous power. Now is the time to leverage that power and take our country back!

But this book isn't just for seniors. All conservatives, of all ages, hold tremendous power. Simply because we have most of the money, start and own most of the businesses, hire and pay the salaries of most of the workforce, do most of the consumer spending.

## WE ARE THE ECONOMIC ENGINE OF AMERICA.

So, why are we getting screwed? Why do we always get the short end of the stick? Why are corporations so quick to disrespect and belittle and offend us? Why aren't they concerned with losing our business? Why aren't they worried they'll lose half or more of their customers?

I know why. Because we've been polite and silent. No more. Now we have to scream and threaten and intimidate just like the left has all these years. Two can play that game. It's time for conservatives, Christians, patriots and Trump deplorables to "model" Jesse Jackson, Al Sharpton, and BLM.

Are you sick and tired of these major corporations, most of them publicly-traded on Wall Street, supporting radical, extreme, anti-American and socialist/Marxist causes?

Are you sick of the big tech overlords cancelling and censoring us because we're conservative, Christian, patriotic Trump voters?

With the help of this book, we're going to fight back, and strike back. We're going to convince these "woke" clueless fools that run the biggest billion dollar companies in America to play fair and respect conservatives, or we will starve them, bankrupt them, and bring them to their knees.

Keep in mind, we're much nicer than Democrats, liberals and assorted socialists, Marxists, communists and America-haters.

They want to ban and censor us. I don't want to stop them from speaking. I want to simply protect free speech in America for everyone.

They want to convince every company to support an extreme, radical, Marxist agenda—supporting open borders, unfettered illegal immigration, no Voter ID (i.e. election fraud), BLM (whose founders proudly admit they're Marxist), Antifa, gun control, unconstitutional lockdowns, vaccine passports, transgender bathrooms and sports teams, restrictions on free speech, Marxist brainwashing in public schools (critical race theory), hatred of America, hatred and defunding of police, and hatred of Israel.

On the other hand, I don't want corporations to support my conservative, patriotic views. I don't want corporations to support the GOP or Trump or secure borders, or Voter ID. I don't want corporations to denounce BLM.

My goal (and I hope your goal too) is just to get these "woke" fools to stay neutral. To stay out of politics. To leave us all alone. Don't pick sides. Stay out of the battle. We'll fight our own battles.

But if these companies make the foolish and tragic mistake of taking sides against us, we will now band together and teach them a lesson they'll never forget. We will bombard them with protests and boycotts (NEVER violence) until they come to their senses, fall to the knees and cry "Uncle."

I'm in a unique position. I am one of America's leading conservative voices. I'm a nationally-syndicated conservative talk show host. My show airs daily from 6 p.m. to 9 p.m. Eastern (3 p.m. to 6 p.m. Pacific), on USA Radio Network. I talk 3 hours a day, 15 hours a week, 60 hours a month, 720 hours a year.

And that's just on my show. I am also a guest for hundreds of media interviews, write hundreds of newspaper columns, and write books. My loud, outspoken, controversial mouth never stops moving 24/7/365.

But after all that talking, I suddenly realized talking isn't enough. We have to take ACTION. "If it is to be, it is up to me."

Remember "Show and Tell" from elementary school? It wasn't about talking. It was about showing through action. We have to take action. We have to show corporations, their CEOs and executives, their Boards of Directors, that we mean business. That we'll put our money where our mouths are.

If they offend, disrespect, or ignore us like we're invisible, we will cut them off at the knees. We are ready and willing to punish them—just like Jesse Jackson, Al Sharpton, BLM, or gay rights activists, or social justice warriors, or environmental activists. Two can play that game.

**From now on, two WILL play that game!**

And I decided I had to make it easy for you. So, I went to my great friend Nicky Billou, and we put together a list of who to contact at the 100+ biggest, most clueless, dumbest, "woke-est" companies in America who dare to offend, disrespect, disregard, or intentionally screw over the Silent Majority.

**We've made it as easy as "A,B,C."**

In this book, we've given you the keys to the kingdom. All the contacts you need are right here. Start mailing, emailing and calling these fools. Remember, no violence, no threats, **ever.**

Never hurt a soul. Never damage anyone's property. **Ever.**

Just give them all a piece of your mind and remind them we can and will make spending decisions based on who respects us versus who screws us over.

It's a new day, a new dawn. From now on, whoever disrespects us, will pay a heavy price. Money talks. And we (the Silent Majority) control a majority of the money. Dare to treat us like crap, and soon these companies may find themselves out of business. Or, if not completely out of business, even if the company survives, certainly these

CEOs who choose to disrespect or offend us, will find themselves out of a job.

We will teach them all a valuable lesson: STAY OUT OF POLITICS. Don't take a side. In capitalism, a company's only jobs are to A) Make money. B) Keep your customers happy. Why would you pick a fight with half of your customers?

We're not asking you to take our side. We can fight our own battles. We don't need you on our side. But don't even think of taking a stand against us. Because we hold all the power. From now on, choose to hurt us, and we will bring you to your knees.

Always remember, WE HAVE THE POWER.

Now for the first time, we must take action and use that power.

# CHAPTER ONE

# WHAT DOES THE SILENT MAJORITY BELIEVE IN?

Here's a lesson in "raw truth" for these woke corporate CEOs and their executive teams and Board of Directors. These big shots live in a "bubble." They know what Wall Street thinks. But they have no clue how Main Street thinks. They're clueless and out of touch. I'm about to educate you. This is how at least half your customers think. It's most probably more than half. It's absolutely 60% or more of the spending on your products—because our half spends most of the money. It might pay to listen and learn.

At least 74 million Americans voted for President Trump. Everyone I know believes that number was actually much higher. I'm guessing Trump really got between 80 and 85 million votes. But we know for a fact a little over 74 million Americans voted for Trump—because that's the number even the biased, fake news, media frauds and B.S. artists count as fact.

This is the "Silent Majority." It's also the base of the Republican Party. And I know what these 74 million (and probably a few million more) voters believe in. How do I know? Because I've tested out my beliefs at dozens of major GOP events in the past six months—where I was the keynote speaker.

The result? I got wild, enthusiastic **STANDING OVATIONS** at all these events.

I know corporate CEOs and Boards have no clue about this. I know the media will be shocked. But what's truly amazing is that the Republican leadership in DC and even the RNC (Republican National Committee) has no clue what their own most loyal, passionate voters believe in.

**But this is the raw truth.**

I'm here to spread the gospel. I'm here to report "the truth will set you free." The American people are desperate to hear the raw truth. It's so rare they ever hear it. This is how you get standing ovations from 80 million+ Republicans, conservatives, Christians, patriots and capitalists.

My message to the GOP leadership in DC: **This is how you win elections.**

And my message to corporations: This is how a majority of your customers think. Maybe you should pay attention. Maybe you should respect their views.

When the mainstream media reads this chapter, they're going to get sick to their stomachs. So is the DC Swamp. And the Deep State. And the entire education system—from public school teacher unions to college professors. And so will 22+ million government employees, bureaucrats and establishment politicians. You all tried to brainwash us. You failed miserably. All of your work 24/7 to deceive and brainwash the American people was for nothing. No one believes your lies and fake news anymore.

I began my speeches with: "Here is what I know. Here is what I believe. Here is raw truth. Let me know if you agree by your applause. Only applaud if you agree."

I said, "No matter what the lying fake news media says, no matter what they try to stuff down our throats, I know President Donald J. Trump won the 2020 election."

**Wild applause.**

"I know Biden and the Democrats rigged, fixed and stole the election."

**Wild applause.**

"I know the more they ban, censor and forbid us from saying Trump won the election, their hysterical, illogical reaction is proof positive they stole it."

**Wild applause.**

"They think they destroyed Trump and demoralized us. The opposite is true. We love Trump now more than ever. We know Trump was one of the greatest presidents in our country's history. And we want him back. We'd walk over hot coals for him. After all your lies, fake news and fake polls, Donald Trump hasn't lost one supporter. And that's precisely why you hate him so much."

**Wild applause.**

"We know the perfect ticket in 2024 is Trump together with Florida Governor Ron DeSantis."

**Wild applause.**

"We know Voter ID isn't 'racist.' We know it's how you rigged and stole the election. With no Voter ID you used millions of fake mail-in ballots to steal the election in key battleground states."

**Wild applause.**

"We know no judge ever looked at the merits of our case. They simply feared for their lives. They knew liberal mobs like BLM and antifa would burn the country down. They knew their own lives and the lives of their families were on the line if they overturned a presidential election. They knew the liberal mobs would try to burn their homes down. Their spouses and kids could never leave the house again without police escort. Judges were scared to death. This was about intimidation, threats of violence, and mob justice."

**Wild applause.**

"We know Biden is not the real President. He's brain-dead. He has dementia. He's a puppet."

**Wild applause.**

Who's in charge? Obama. He's back to finish the job. This is Obama's third term as president. But this time he can throw caution to the wind. He can do it in the shadows with brain-dead puppet Biden as the front man. This time Obama has done more damage in the first six months than in his first two terms combined."

**Wild applause.**

"And who is giving the orders to Obama and Biden? China and the Chinese Communist Party controls Obama, Biden, Biden's family, and the Democrat Party." It's all about the money.

**Wild applause.**

"And we know the Mexican Drug Cartels are in charge of border and immigration policy. Democrat politicians are getting wealthy with bribes in offshore accounts deposited by the Mexican Drug Cartels and the Chinese Communist Party."

**Wild applause.**

"And let's not forget Iran. John Kerry and the Democrats are desperate to re-start the Iran treaty. Why? I'll bet my life savings they're all being bribed with billion dollar kickbacks in offshore accounts. These people are selling out America to get rich. They are traitors."

**Wild applause.**

"This is the most radical agenda in history. This is a communist takeover of the United States. The people running our country, hate our country."

**Wild applause.**

"We know the Democrat (ie communist) game plan to destroy the USA is about open borders. They're inviting the entire world in. They want to destroy America, wipe out our votes, and make America foreign to Americans."

**Wild applause.**

"I know the next 9-11 terrorist attack is on the way through that open border with Mexico. I know Covid and third world disease is also coming through that open border. I know a massive violent crime wave is coming through that border. I know that everyone coming through that border wants cradle-to-grave welfare, food stamps and free healthcare. This will collapse our economy. It's the end of America."

**Wild applause.**

"And I know what we must do with traitors who are destroying our country, opening the borders to criminals, disease and debt. LOCK THEM UP. LOCK THEM UP. LOCK THEM UP."

**Wild applause & STANDING OVATION.**

"Who opens the borders in the middle of a deadly pandemic and ships illegal alien invaders across the country into our communities? Traitors who want to destroy our country."

**Wild applause.**

"We know the truth. You can never brainwash us. We will never stop fighting. We will never, ever, ever, give up, or give in. We will take our country back. God bless President Trump. God bless America."

**STANDING OVATION.**

Whether the GOP leadership in DC understands it, or not, **THAT** is what 74 million (or more) GOP voters believe in. That's raw truth that Republican voters are desperate to hear. Only the truth will save America. Only the truth will set us free.

That is how you get a standing ovation from Republican voters. And that is how the GOP wins elections again.

But this lesson isn't just for the GOP leadership and GOP politicians. For the purposes of this book, it's a lesson for corporate America. It's in your interest to understand and accept that half or more of your customers believe in these truths—whether you do, or not. If you offend us, disrespect us, ignore us, or screw us over, you will pay. Our money is as good as the money spent by the radical socialists, Marxists, communists and America-haters on the left.

As a matter of fact, we spend more, likely a lot more than they do. Simply because we do all the work, own all the businesses. We're not illegal aliens, ex-felons, or welfare queens. We make most of the money, so quite naturally we spend most of the money. Pay attention. Don't offend us. We're no longer going to take your abuse. The tide has turned. "If you act woke, you will go broke."

**That's what this book is all about.**

# CHAPTER TWO

# YES, DEMOCRATS STOLE THE 2020 ELECTION

Here's how you know democrats rigged and stole the 2020 election. Let me put this in terms even Democrats can understand.

Let's say a white police officer killed an innocent black man who did nothing wrong. Unlike George Floyd, he had not committed any crime; was not resisting arrest; his body wasn't filled with fentanyl; he had no lifelong violent crime record. None of that. Assume this poor guy was a law-abiding, tax-paying, church-going American. And the white cop killed him for the crime of "driving while black."

What's the reaction of the police? They say the shooting was righteous. They refuse to investigate. There is a bodycam videotape, but they refuse to release it. And get this—they refuse to allow anyone to even talk about it. If any cop talks about it, he loses his job. If anyone in the black community talks about it, social media will suspend them, or ban them for life.

What would all of that mean to you? Guilty as charged, right? The police must be covering up a crime. No one who's innocent acts like that, right?

Guess what? That's the **EXACT** reaction (or should I say, over-reaction) by liberals, Democrats and assorted socialists and communists to Republican accusations of massive voter fraud in the 2020 presidential election.

I thought in America we were all allowed to have our opinion. I thought we had free speech. I thought we had a right to investigate. I thought we had a right to see the videotapes. I thought we had a right to forensic audits.

**I was wrong.**

The fix is in. It's crystal clear to me now, not only was the election rigged, but so is the post-election. It's simple psychology. Just look at the absurd reaction, or over-reaction by Democrats.

Would anyone dare ban the right to discuss a possible racist police killing? Can you imagine the reaction by liberals, black activists and the ACLU? What if the Minneapolis police permanently banned any discussion of the George Floyd death? What if every black American who tried to give their opinion on Twitter, Facebook or YouTube was banned for life?

Who acts like that? Only guilty people.

**That's how you know.**

Here's the questions I want answered…

If Democrats didn't rig and steal the election, why are they so afraid of forensic audits in key battleground states—specifically the audit in places like Arizona and Georgia (and many more likely to come)?

When Trump was an 8 to 1 landslide favorite with bettors around the world late on election night and clearly headed to a landslide electoral victory, why did five states suddenly announce (in coordination) they were stopping counting for the night?

How come by morning these states had resumed counting with no GOP witnesses, and suddenly Biden was ahead? I thought they stopped counting?

How come Michigan had a dump of 149,772 votes at 6:31 AM on November 4th —with 96% of the vote going to Biden?

How did Wisconsin find 143,379 votes at 3:42 a.m. on November 4th, just about all of them for Biden? How come you could only produce numbers like this for Biden with no GOP witnesses in the room?

How come in Philadelphia Democrats were so desperate to keep Republican witnesses out of the counting room? Why did you refuse entry of Republican witnesses, even with a court order in hand?

In Detroit, why did you cover the windows of the vote counting room with pizza boxes, so no Republican could see in?

Why are there are videotapes of vans in Detroit pulling up in the middle of the night with boxes of thousands of ballots? How could those ballots be counted after Midnight of Election Night?

In Atlanta, there are videotapes of suitcases with thousands of fake ballots suddenly appearing, only after a fake water main break was used to force all GOP witnesses out of the counting room. Why can't we discuss these videotapes?

How come Twitter banned me (Wayne Allyn Root) for life over mentioning these videotapes?

How come in Arizona the audit director says Dominion refuses to comply with a subpoena and turn over the password to their voting machines?

How come the Biden DOJ wants to stop the Arizona audit?

These are all valid questions. Why aren't we allowed to ask them? To discuss them? To post them on social media? What are Democrats hiding? What are they so afraid of?

In the end, **that's** the proof Democrats rigged and stole the 2020 presidential election. I knew it on Election Night at 1 AM EST, when Trump was pulling away with a landslide electoral win, and five states all announced at the same time they were stopping counting, for the first time in history. I knew then. Everyone with a brain knew then.

But it's now twice as clear that the election was stolen by simply seeing the ridiculous, heavy-handed over-reaction by Democrats when we try to do forensic audits. Only guilty people are afraid of the light. Only guilty people won't let you search their home without a warrant.

That's the "tell." That gives it all away. That's how you know it really was rigged and stolen. Because Democrats are so desperate to stop you from looking at the election, auditing the ballots, or even talking about it.

**Democrats are guilty as sin.**

# CHAPTER THREE

# FIRST DEMOCRATS STOLE THE ELECTION, NOW THEY'RE TRYING TO STEAL THE COUNTRY

This is the most important thing I've ever written.

This is my chance to play the modern-day version of Paul Revere. "The commies are coming. The commies are coming." Yes, I am reporting a communist takeover. But the leader of this attack is not who it appears to be.

Republicans, Conservatives, patriots and capitalists are sick right about now. We're in shock. We can't believe Trump isn't president. We can't believe Americans voted against the greatest economy, perhaps in history. And the greatest jobs picture ever. And the greatest improvement in middle class incomes ever. And after the Covid lockdown and economic collapse, Trump produced the greatest economic comeback ever. Remember 33% GDP in Q3 2020? That was the biggest number in history. Who would vote against all that? You'd have to be self-hating and suicidal.

We also can't believe America voted for a feeble old man with dementia who mumbles "I don't know what I'm signing, but I'm gonna sign these Executive Orders." And who says "There was no vaccine before I became president." Even though he got his two vaccine shots before he became president. The man is brain dead. His head is hollowed out. He's a walking zombie.

We all believe the election was rigged and stolen. We all know the feeble old man now called "President" would be more at home in a nursing home, than the White House. That man can't be our new president.

I have news for my fellow conservatives, Republicans, capitalists and patriots. Biden's not president. He's a puppet. Yes, we have a new president. But his name is…

**Barack Obama.**

Admit it. Now that I've said it out loud, it all makes sense. Obama is the real president, back for his third term, to finish the job.

Biden's job was to stand there and look moderate, and credible, and reasonable. So as not to scare the voters. Democrats could never have won the election with a radical, extreme, America-hating candidate. They had to run a puppet who appeared "moderate." But Biden isn't the real president. Obama is the man behind the throne. Obama is the real president.

Look at the radical Executive Orders that Biden issued on his first day in office, the most in history. They all sound like Obama wrote them. This third term is "Obama Unmasked." With Biden as the front man, Obama can finally be himself. Obama is able to do all the radical things he never dared do as the actual president.

Look at a few of Biden's executive orders and new laws and policies proposed...

- Open borders. No more wall. Everyone gets in, during a pandemic, with no testing for Covid. Illegal alien felons must be released from jail. Halt to deportations. Full legalization for millions of alien lawbreakers. Include illegal aliens in the US census. Once into the country, give them the right to bring all their relatives in too, with no requirement for education, skills or background checks. Ban the use of the word "illegal alien."

- Make every action and economic policy about "racism" "social justice" and "racial equity." Even climate change is about "racism."

- Re-start the Iranian nuclear treaty. Give murdering Mullahs everything they ever dreamed of, and then some, endanger our best friend Israel's existence, and get absolutely nothing in return. And for good measure, wait over a month to call Israel's Prime Minister, so the whole world knows we no longer have Israel's back.

- Kill the lucrative US energy industry and make us dependent on foreign oil from our enemies again. Kill the Keystone Pipeline. Kill oil, coal, natural gas, fracking, even permits for drilling. Re-enter the Paris Climate Agreement that kills all our jobs, while allowing China to pollute all it wants. This will decimate our economy and make us dependent on the same kind of green energy that caused the meltdown in Texas this past winter. Don't forget gas lines and $5 to $7 a gallon gas. Oh right, we already had that in month four of the young Biden presidency.

- Kiss China's ass. Give China every advantage they ever dreamed of. Damage the US economy with taxes and regulations and the Green New Deal. Open the borders. Pile up the debt. End the trade war with China. Give China access to the US energy grid. And get this one, ban the use of the term "China virus." Hard to believe this is actually a Biden Executive Order, not a segment of "Saturday Night Live." Under Biden (or in reality, Obama), China is eating our lunch.

Even the players in Biden's cabinet and staff are all Obama re-treads. Almost a 100% match.

Trust me, I'm Obama's Columbia college classmate. I know how he thinks. I understand his plan. This has Obama's fingerprints all over it. This is the Cloward-Piven plan we learned at Columbia University, almost 40 years ago.

This is the 3$^{rd}$ term of Obama. In his first two terms Obama tried his best to destroy the economy, high-paying jobs, healthcare, the US energy industry, the great American middle class, our relationship with Israel, American exceptionalism, and capitalism itself. He damaged us badly, but he fell short.

Now Obama's back to finish the job.

# CHAPTER FOUR

# NOW THEY'RE TRYING TO STEAL THE COUNTRY – PART II

This is Part Deux on the Communist Takeover of the United States. Part I centered on the new President who oversees it all—Barack Obama. I do believe the new president is in fact, the old president. This is the third term of Obama.

Obama gave it his best shot. He crippled America, but he couldn't quite finish the job. He needed Hillary to be elected to finish the job, but we all know how that turned out. Trump managed to beat a rigged election by bringing out the biggest turnout of white middle class voters in history. Obama vowed to never let that happen again.

Hence the election of old, weak, feeble, brain-dead Basement Biden—hopelessly lost and confused with dementia. He's fallen and he can't get up. Obama likes it that way. Biden is Obama's puppet and front guy. Obama can now finish the job and do it under the cover of darkness.

Biden gives him "cover." Now Obama can carry out his plan more ruthlessly than he ever could when he was the first black president, and wanted to convince American voters he wasn't "radical" or "extreme." Back then, Obama had to move with caution. He had to "boil the frog slowly"—as I warned in my #1 national bestseller in 2013 "The Ultimate Obama Survival Guide."

All that is history. No more moving with caution. See Biden's record-setting Executive Orders. They are as radical and Marxist as anything ever seen in America's history. Obama is running the show. He is back to finish the job he started in 2008.

Here in Part II, I will explain **the actual plan**. I learned it at Columbia University from 1979 to 1983. I was Obama's college classmate at the Ivy League college where Marxism and the destruction of America was taught in every classroom. The plan was called Cloward-Piven, named after a husband-wife team of Columbia professors.

Cloward and Piven created the perfect Marxist plan: get every American possible on welfare and other government handout programs, in order to overwhelm the system, bring the national debt to levels never imagined, bankrupt America, and bring business owners to their knees when the economy collapses. Then you've got a socialist country.

I recognize exactly what's happening today in America with Biden as PINO (president in name only). Obama is running the show and he's using a modified version of the Cloward and Piven plan from our Columbia days.

Democrats (aka socialists, Marxists, communists) tried to get everyone on welfare for the past 38 years since Obama and I graduated Columbia. They came close, but they never could never quite overwhelm and collapse the system. The success of capitalism, Reagan and Trump got in the way.

But now Obama has the modified the plan. He is going to use the next four years to open the borders and MAFA (Make America Foreign Again). This is a modified version of Cloward-Piven. If you can't get every American on welfare...

**Then change the composition of America.**

Open the borders and recruit millions, eventually tens of millions, of foreigners who don't speak English;

who know nothing about American history, or the US Constitution; who have no education, talent or skills; who require cradle to grave welfare; who will vote Democrat forever more, in order to keep the welfare checks coming.

Soon, America is so filled with foreigners, America becomes foreign to Americans. And those foreigners tip the scale and overwhelm the system with all their welfare, food stamps, free healthcare, free education, and a thousand other needs.

Have you seen Biden's Executive Actions? Have you closely watched Biden's first six months in office? It's all dedicated to open borders. It's an obsession. It's all about illegal aliens. He's inviting the whole world into our country. It's about giving them every form of welfare imaginable. It's about giving them rights, privileges and advantages American-born citizens don't have.

This is the Cloward-Piven plan Obama and I learned at Columbia, modified and updated for 2021 by Obama. He's overwhelming the system and collapsing the US economy by flooding our nation will illegal aliens. The floodgates are open. The disaster has begun.

CHAPTER FIVE

# I KNOW WHAT CHINA DID

I don't mean to say, "I told you so." But…

I told you so.

Check the records. Check the archives of my national radio show, "Wayne Allyn Root: Raw & Unfiltered" on USA Radio Network. Check my hundreds of newspaper columns and online commentaries. I said from day one, from early March 2020, as we knew a deadly pandemic was headed our way, that this China Flu (aka Covid-19) was man-made in a Chinese bio-warfare lab in Wuhan.

I also reported it appeared likely Dr. Anthony Fauci had used American taxpayer money to fund the creation of Covid-19.

And I predicted we were experiencing a massive cover-up by China, the Chinese Communist Party, the WHO, the CDC and Dr. Fauci, simply because they'd all be on the hook for trillions of dollars in damages caused by their evil invention. They funded it, they own it. The only way out for them was a worldwide coverup.

But suddenly as I finish writing this book, everyone is admitting this deadly pandemic is almost certainly man-made from a Chinese bio-warfare lab. Thanks guys, "welcome to my world." You're a year and a half late.

So, since my gut about the origins of the China Flu was right on the money for 15 months now, while everyone else was blind, deaf and really dumb, what else am I right about? is it possible my second prediction is on the money too?

Because I've said all along this was no mistake, this was no coincidence, this wasn't bad fortune. This was—from day one—a purposeful attack on the United States by China.

In my opinion, there are only two possibilities to why and how this pandemic happened. Either way, China is guilty of the worst act of mass murder since Hitler, Stalin and China's Mao Zedong.

First, behind door number one, it's possible the China Flu virus escaped out of a Wuhan bio-warfare lab. But that's not an "accident." China developed this as a bio-warfare weapon of mass destruction. Even if it got out by accident, they are responsible for the deaths of millions.

But it's much worse than that. Once it was out and Chinese officials knew, they made the deadly decision to let thousands of infected Chinese board flights to America and other Western countries to spread the pandemic worldwide. They clearly believed in Rahm Emanuel's famous saying, "Never let a crisis go to waste."

But the choice behind door number two is even more evil. Did China *purposely* send this biowarfare weapon of mass destruction to America to end the trade war, and as a bonus, destroy us, our economy and President Trump, all in one?

My gut says look behind door number two. I believe this was a purposeful attack upon America. I don't believe it was a mistake, or coincidence. Look at the timing. Look what China achieved.

This pandemic just happened to wipe out Trump's economy—the greatest economy in modern history. Overnight America went from prosperity to what amounted to a Great Depression. The stock market collapsed. Millions of small businesses were closed. Millions of Americans lost their jobs and a large portion of their lifesavings.

We added trillions in debt to pay for the stimulus, bailouts and corporate welfare needed to prop up the economy. This debt will weaken our economy for decades to come. Someday soon, it may collapse our economy.

In addition, many of the structural problems from the China Flu pandemic remain. Supply chains are destroyed. Massive hyper-inflation is here. Gas prices, food prices, home prices, ammo prices are through the roof. The middle class is decimated. America's famous work ethic has been destroyed. We have a massive worker shortage. No business can find enough employees. Many businesses are closing because of this drastic worker shortage.

Under Trump, we had re-established our economic dominance in the world. China was the biggest loser. Now it's all reversed. Guess who's back in the driver's seat? China. What a coincidence. It was their pandemic. Yet somehow they came out the biggest winner.

The China Flu pandemic changed everything. It allowed Democrats to cheat, rig and steal a presidential election with millions of mail-in ballots, no Voter ID, no signature verification, ballot harvesting and ballots counted days after the election was over.

Suddenly Biden was president, a man I believe is clearly owned lock, stock and barrel by the Chinese

Communist Party. What a coincidence. I may have been born yesterday, but I wasn't born in the past five minutes. I smell a rat.

His first day as president Biden showed his cards by banning the use of the word "China Flu." Really? How bizarre is that? They don't even care if we know Biden is owned by the CCP. They're laughing at us out in the open, for all to see.

Suddenly the trade war is over and forgotten. The borders are wide open. China is making hundreds of billions on human trafficking, sex trafficking, and the manufacture of fentanyl and opioids smuggled across a porous U.S.-Mexico border.

And if WWIII ever breaks out between the United States and China, wouldn't China love it if our military was weakened? Well don't look now, but under puppet President Biden (and real President Obama) the US military's stated #1 priority is rooting out white supremacists (ie anyone registered Republican who loves this country). The stated #2 priority is protecting gay and transgender rights. Don't forget BLM and gay pride flags are flying at US embassies around the world.

China is laughing at us. Chinese leaders are high fiving. This is China's greatest dream. They've installed a president who is destroying the U.S. military. Instead of new tanks, or warships, or stealth bombers, our military is spending our money on sex change operations for transgender soldiers.

Good luck to the U.S. in a war versus 1.4 billion Chinese focused only on the destruction of the USA. No distractions allowed for the Chinese military. No transgenders either.

The debate is over. China developed Covid-19 in a bio-warfare lab as a weapon of mass destruction. The only question to investigate now is, did they send it our way purposefully. That's the $10 trillion question.

Either way, I believe China is guilty of the worst act of mass murder since Hitler, Stalin and China's Mao Zedong.

But they'll never pay for their war crimes because they have installed a puppet president in the White House. I believe puppet President Biden (and real President Obama) are owned lock, stock and barrel by the Chinese Communist Party.

This is why we are experiencing a communist takeover. This was China's plan. China executed it brilliantly, from the pandemic to the presidency. China is in charge. And for the first time since 1776, America is in grave danger of being destroyed from within.

# CHAPTER SIX

# THE MURDER OF THE MIDDLE CLASS

Back in 2014, I wrote a book titled, "The Murder of the Middle Class." Don't look now, but it's happening.

Back then I was referring primarily to the murder of middle-class jobs and the American Dream. Today it's literally MURDER. Democrats appear to want the middle class eliminated. They're not just after our jobs, they're playing "Russian Roulette" with our lives.

If you think I'm kidding, or being sarcastic, think again. I'm dead serious (excuse the pun). Biden, or more likely the real decision-makers behind a man that resembles a brain-dead puppet, really do appear to be carrying out "the murder of the middle class."

Let's start with Covid. If Covid is as bad as Democrats make it out to be; if we're all at risk of death; if the entire country needs to be shutdown, locked down, masked, distanced and vaccinated forever more; then why are Democrats letting thousands of strangers a day into our country? We know nothing about them, or their health.

Why aren't they testing them for Covid and other third world diseases, and if sick, sending them back? Just like we did for decades at Ellis Island. Why would anyone want to risk allowing sick or diseased people into the USA?

Based on the numbers at the border so far this year, we can expect between one million and two million illegal aliens entering our country over just the next year to spread infection and death, and quite possibly re-ignite a pandemic that almost took down our entire economy. Who would allow this? Who would encourage it? Only someone looking to destroy the USA, US economy and the great American middle class.

Wait, it gets much worse. These illegal aliens, many of them diseased, or sick with Covid, are being put on airplanes—without any ID. We don't know who they are, where they're from, or why they're here. What if they're sitting next to you and your children on a plane? They could make you sick, they could kill your spouse or children with Covid, or one of the new variant strains from Brazil, UK, South Africa, India, or any other third world disease.

Or they could kill you, your family and everyone else on that plane in a terrorist attack. How does the Biden Administration know who is a terrorist? They don't. And obviously they don't care.

But wait, it gets worse. A fan of mine was recently headed to Texas for business. She couldn't find a hotel room at any moderately priced hotel in Dallas-Ft Worth. Most of the hotels around Dallas (and the rest of Texas) are booked by the government. Why is the US government buying up most of the hotel rooms in Texas? They're housing illegal aliens in nice hotel suites—with our tax dollars. Don't take my word for it. Even USA Today reported Hiltons, Marriotts, Comfort Suites, TownPlace Suites, and Homewood Suites (among others) were booked up by the Biden government to house illegal aliens.

Good luck finding a hotel room in Texas if you're an American citizen. But of course, that's not the big problem. How many of these illegal alien hotel guests have Covid? How many have actually been tested? Biden & Co are sending potentially diseased foreigners into US hotels. They could sicken or kill the other guests. They could certainly sicken or kill the hotel staff. And all these sick American citizens could take Covid back home to their families, workplaces and schools. But I'm guessing this is happening in ever border state.

Folks, this is insanity. This is reckless manslaughter. Biden and his American-hating, socialist cabal are playing "Russian Roulette" with our lives. They obviously couldn't care less if American citizens die, as long as the ends justify the means (as Marxist author Saul Alinsky taught them).

What is that end goal? Democrats want to flood America, and in particular Texas, with illegal aliens, otherwise known in Democrat circles as "future Democrat voters." They want to change the electorate. They want to replace American voters with foreign voters, dependent on welfare from cradle to grave.

They want to "fundamentally change America" with one party rule. They want to make sure only Democrats will be able to win elections. They want to make America foreign to Americans.

And to make this goal a reality, it sure looks like they're willing to carry out "the Murder of the Middle Class."

# CHAPTER SEVEN

# FORGET UNITY.
# WE ARE "THE RESISTANCE"

Remember the old New Orleans Saints head coach Jim Mora who went nuts at a press conference? "Playoffs? Playoffs? Don't talk about playoffs! Are you kidding me?"

I have my own version of those words by Jim Mora: "Unity? Unity? Are you freakin' kidding me? Don't talk about unity."

Joe Biden can mouth the word 'unity' all he wants. It's a lie. Democrats don't want unity. They want to censor us, ban us, purge us, wipe away American history like it never happened, and then intimidate us into meekly going along with it all. They want us kneeling and saying "thank you" while they destroy America and our American way of life. That's what they mean by "unity." They want us to sit back and say nothing in the name of unity, while they destroy our jobs, freedoms and way of life. So, quote me: "You can take your unity and shove it where the sun don't shine."

Got it?

I won't even discuss the statements by liberals and Democrat politicians that sounded like acts of war. I won't get into how they drag conservatives and of course, white males, into the gutter. I won't get into the way they slander us, attack us, denigrate us, slime us, and aim hate speech at us.

I'm a S.O.B. (son of a butcher). My butcher father had great common sense. He taught me to "watch what a man does, not what he says." So, I'll just point out President Biden's first acts as president. These were literally the first things he did as soon as he moved into the White House, so they must be the most important to him.

• Biden had a record-setting first day in office. In a matter of hours, he killed between 70,000 and 100,000 jobs. He killed the Keystone Pipeline. He halted all oil and gas permits on federal land. He halted construction of the US-Mexico border wall.

These weren't just any jobs Biden killed on day one as president. These were high-paying middle-class jobs in construction and energy. And ironically, these were union jobs. This will be a disaster for the US economy. Most of those wonderful blue-collar workers are now unemployed and on welfare and food stamps.

• Biden offered up a radical amnesty plan for every illegal alien in the United States. Biden announced he wants to give every illegal alien inside the USA a fast-track to citizenship in only eight years. This is a disaster for America in many ways.

First, this radical amnesty plan rewards law-breakers. The rule of law and US Constitution no longer matter. We're not America anymore, we're "Mad Max."

Second, these new law-breakers-turned-citizens will become 23 million new Democrat voters (a Harvard study reported there are 23 million illegal aliens in the USA). Republicans will never win again.

That's what this is about. Trust me, if there were 23 million European white Christians and Israeli Jews trying to illegally enter the USA through the open Mexican border, Democrats would fund and build the wall in a week! They'd probably add a moat with alligators!

Third, these millions of illegals-turned-citizens will take millions of jobs from American citizens. And lower the wages of millions more.

Fourth these new citizens will bankrupt America as they all qualify for welfare, food stamps, free Obamacare and 100 other welfare programs.

Fifth, they will overcrowd and bankrupt our public schools and healthcare system.

Sixth, they will overwhelm the police, courts, and prison system.

Seventh, this "amnesty" will encourage tens of millions of additional foreigners to invade our border. Soon none of us will recognize America. This will be a country foreign to Americans.

Lastly, Biden will have to dramatically raise taxes on American citizens and business owners to pay for this massive cost.

• Biden also froze deportation of illegal aliens scheduled to be kicked out of our country. How many American citizens will die because illegal alien felons were allowed to stay?

• Biden required non-citizens to be included in the Census—thereby increasing funding to Sanctuary cities and broke Democrat welfare states, while adding new Democrat Congressman to cities and states filled with illegal aliens.

• Biden reversed the Trump travel ban on passport holders from seven terrorist-friendly countries. Just what the American people desperately need—more visitors from Yemen, Somalia and Iran. I can't wait.

• Biden rejoined the Paris Climate Accord and promised to add thousands of new environmental regulations. This will destroy manufacturing and energy companies, kill millions of high-paying jobs and dramatically raise energy bills on the middle class.

Biden's day one priority was forcing women's sports to allow biologically male transgender athletes to compete in girl's sports, use girl's bathrooms, and dress in girl's locker rooms. This is a declaration of war on women—even if liberal mothers are too blinded by feminism, atheism, communism and dumb political correctness to see it.

Biden is not a "moderate." He is either a radical Marxist out to destroy America, or a feeble old man with dementia, being used as a puppet by George Soros, Barack Obama, Valerie Jarrett, Nancy Pelosi, AOC, Ilhan Omar, and the CCP (Chinese Communist Party) to destroy this country. But it really doesn't matter. Either way he's leading us down the road to disaster, ruin, misery and poverty. Biden (or O'Biden—with Obama pulling the strings) is going to turn America into Venezuela.

This isn't "unity." It's the destruction of America and everything that ever made it great. I'm not in unity. Are you?

**Count me as "the Resistance."**

# CHAPTER EIGHT

# WHAT'S THE GAME PLAN?

I repeat: "WE HAVE THE POWER." Now we have to use it. This book puts the power in your hands. We've made it so easy. We've done the major research, homework and groundwork for you. It's all laid out here for you. We've provided the names, phone numbers, physical addresses and email addresses.

Now all you have to do is "Dial for Dollars." Just start making your opinions known to the decision-makers at all the companies listed in this book. This is how we take back the USA, one company at a time.

Let these woke morons know they're going to lose your business, they're going to lose your dollars, and they're going to lose their jobs. They're going to kill the goose that laid the golden egg.

Tell them to stay out of politics altogether. But certainly, stay far away from any endorsement of radical, extreme, leftist, anti-American politics. And most importantly, stop offending, intimidating and bullying conservatives and patriots like you and me. We are their customers too. And we are far more important customers than the "progressives" on the left who happen to scream the loudest. We have the most purchasing power. We spend the most money.

**Now it's time for conservatives, Christians, Trump deplorables, and patriots to scream, protest and boycott as loudly as the angry left.**

As Founding Father Benjamin Franklin, one of courageous heroes of the American Revolution, said in 1776, "We must all hang together, or, most assuredly, we shall all hang separately."

We can do this. You've got this. It's time to bring out "your inner Jesse Jackson and Al Sharpton." It's time to hold your boot against the necks of corporate America. Make them feel the heat. Put their feet to the fire. Make them understand they either get out of the way, get out of politics, or face the wrath of the Silent Majority.

Jesse Jackson and Al Sharpton both used threats (not violent ones, only economic ones), protests and boycotts to change the direction and behavior of corporate America.

We can use our economic power to bring the pendulum back towards conservatism, capitalism and patriotism.

It's already working. Look at attendance and ratings for sports like NBA, NFL, MLB—all dramatically down since the disastrous kneeling for our national anthem and statements by players in support of BLM. Those sports have been crushed by the Silent Majority. They've cost themselves billions of dollars. Pure stupidity. Self-destructive. Business suicide. An economic death-wish.

Look at the Oscars, Emmys, Grammys, ESPYS—you name the awards show. Ratings are in the tank. All-time lows. No one is watching anymore. Will the last viewer please turn off the lights. The clueless out-of-touch idiots of Hollywood, movies, television, music and sports have damaged and destroyed their own revenue streams. Crazy. "Stupid is, as stupid does."

Look at CNN. Ratings are off by 70% since the election. But all the TV news ratings are down. They got what they wished for. No Trump, no ratings. How stupid are these people?

Everything liberals touch, they destroy. Look at every major urban inner city in America. Hiroshima looks better today than many of America's inner cities. The Japanese rebuilt after the atomic bomb blasts. Meanwhile we destroyed ourselves from within by electing Democrats to run our big cities. No nuclear bombs were needed. Just put moronic, corrupt, insane, self-destructive, Marxist suicide bombers, masquerading as "Democrats who care about fairness, equality and social justice" in charge. Voila. Instant Hiroshima.

What's that old wisdom, "It aint over until the fat lady sings." It's the ninth inning, and we're behind. But it isn't over yet. We've only just begun to fight.

I hope this book is the perfect tool in your hands. We've done the groundwork. All you have to do it start dialing and writing (emails, or physical letters). Lots of them.

Set aside ten to twenty minutes a day. Maybe early each morning at 6 a.m. before work. Maybe late each evening at 11 p.m. after work, when the kids are asleep. But please set aside just a few minutes every day (or as often as possible) to make your conservative, Christian and patriotic opinions felt and heard.

I know we can still save the greatest country in world history, ever blessed by God. I will be relentless. I will never, ever, ever, ever give up. I will fight like a cornered wolverine. I will do more than just talking (even though I talk for a living). I will take concrete action. And I will pray. How about you?

Start "dialing for dollars." If 74+ million Trump warriors use the list inside this book relentlessly, we can claw back what's our birthright. We can take back this nation. We can protect capitalism. We can protect economic, personal and religious freedom. And protect our children's future.

If the greatest country in world history is worth fighting for, even dying for, then it has to be worth making a few phone calls and writing a few emails each day, right?

We've lost a few battles, mainly because we've been silent, we haven't spoken loudly enough, we haven't taken action. But I have faith we can still win the war. We just have to get as angry, loud, pushy and intimidating as the left. Model them. Use their tactics. Beat 'em at their own game. That's why we wrote this book. That's why we did all this research for you. That's why you bought this book.

Now get to work! Fight relentlessly. Never ever, ever, give up. We have a great nation and our childrens' future to save.

**God Bless America.**

**Wayne Allyn Root**
**ROOTforAmerica.com**
**WayneRoot@gmail.com**

# CHAPTER NINE

# POST SCRIPT
## JULY 4, 2021

Just as I was finishing this book with my great pal Nicky, two American companies committed suicide. These two companies are like Vegas blinking neon signs proving why we wrote this book. I wrote a newspaper column about it for July 4th. I had to share it. This column explains the reason for this entire book. Here it is. Enjoy.

### This Independence Day, Tell Corporate America to Shut Up and Stop Committing Suicide

*By Wayne Allyn Root*

This is stupidity. This is insanity. This is suicide. American companies and institutions are purposely destroying themselves. They're ripping apart billion-dollar brands that have taken decades of hard work to build. And they're doing it in a matter of days.

They're marching off cliffs like sheep.

Keep in mind sheep are pretty darn dumb. They can't think for themselves. If one sheep walks off a cliff, they'll all happily follow. Did you ever imagine CEOs of billion-dollar companies could be as dumb as sheep?

Who committed suicide this week? Two of the biggest brand names in America...

Let's start with Victoria's Secret. I have a secret for them. You just killed your business. How clueless can you get? Victoria's Secret sells lingerie, bras, bathing suits. This isn't brain surgery. Those products are sold by beautiful female models. Always have been, always will be. They're so beautiful they're called "Angels." And here's a secret for clueless Victoria's Secret: men open up their wallets for beautiful women.

Most women want to look like angels too. Even if only for one night with dim lights on. Even if only while wearing Victoria's Secret lingerie.

Sex and beauty sell clothing. All clothing, but especially women's clothing. And really, really, especially, lingerie, bras and bathing suits.

But the brains of Victoria's Secret executives have clearly been eaten by zombies, or brainwashed by woke, liberal, feminist fools. They've decided to fire all their sexy, gorgeous, skinny, busty models. The angels are being replaced by overweight, unattractive, feminist icons and transgender models.

Even if you personally believe this leftist, feminist drivel, that's fine. Be a Stepford Wife in private. But to attach this insanity to your billion-dollar brand is suicide. No one will buy clothing, let alone bras, panties and lingerie from unattractive, overweight feminists and transgender models. Your business is ruined, thanks to your radical, absurd, insane political philosophy.

But the NFL could be even stupider and more reckless than Victoria's Secret. Have you seen the latest TV ad for the NFL? It says, "The NFL is gay, lesbian, bisexual and transgender." Insanity does not even begin to describe how clueless this is.

I'm Exhibit A. I'm the prototype for your typical NFL fan.

I've loved the NFL since I was five years old. I live for Sundays to watch NFL football. I live and die with my Dallas Cowboys. I love America, faith, family, freedom, my fiancé, and my NFL. That's not a brand. That's a religion! The NFL is part of my life. It's the DNA of America.

Why would the NFL ruin their brand by getting involved with politics? And not just any politics, but the most controversial and radical politics possible.

First you damaged your NFL brand with kneeling for the national anthem. Then you supported BLM rioting, looting and burning. Very bad decisions. Ratings dramatically declined. Now this. Are you trying to alienate 60% or more of your most loyal fans? Why would a billion-dollar brand want to commit suicide?

The NFL is about sports, gambling and violence. It's a perfect mix that attracts mostly macho, straight males. A majority of whom are conservative, Christian, and unabashed patriots. I'd bet my life's fortune that a large majority of the fans sitting in the stands at NFL games voted for President Trump.

Like it, or not, that's your audience. Like it, or not, a majority of the NFL's paying customers have conservative views and values. They go to church, they believe in God, they own guns, they vote Republican, and they idolize Clint Eastwood, Sylvester Stallone and Donald Trump.

Why offend your customers? Why get involved in politics at all? But if you do, why pick a stand that alienates a majority of your most loyal fans? I have nothing against lesbians, or bi-sexuals, or transsexuals, but how many of these groups live and die for NFL football? How many gays, bisexuals, lesbians and transgenders grew up playing football? How many pay for NFL season tickets? Maybe a few dozen in a stadium that seats 75,000? I'm being charitable.

Is the NFL trying to attract .0000000001% new fans, while driving away 60% of their current fans, forever? Is that a smart business decision? Actually, this is business suicide.

The NFL shouldn't hate gays, lesbians or transgenders. I don't. I couldn't care less what your sex, or sexual preference is. Do what you want in the privacy of your bedroom. But what does anyone's sexual choice have to do with football? If the NFL now celebrates BLM and lesbians, will there be TV ads celebrating white people and straight males? If not, why not? Isn't it "racist" to exclude one group? How is it "diversity" to celebrate everyone except white straight males? Seems like a clear cut case of racism, bias, prejudice and intolerance to me.

Will the NFL celebrate straight male pride month? Will future NFL television ads say "We are macho, straight, Republican and proud"? I doubt it. But why not? Since that's your main audience, since that's actually who buys the tickets, that would make the most sense.

Of course, I'm joking. I'm being a wise-ass. I don't want to celebrate white day, or BLM day, or Jewish day, or trans day. I don't believe the NFL should be involved in dividing and polarizing the USA. The NFL should be about sports. Period.

There aren't white fans, or black fans. They're aren't trans or bisexual fans. There are only NFL fans.

The lesson for corporations is, stay out of politics. Don't take sides. Unless you have a business death wish. Unless you want to kill your brand.

This Independence Day, tell corporate America to shut up and stop committing suicide.

CHAPTER TEN

# AN IMMIGRANT'S PERSPECTIVE

*By Nicky Billou, Co-Author*

I was born in the Middle East, a Christian in a country that was over 99.5% Muslim. Growing up, my family and I faced religious and ethnic discrimination every single day. When the Islamic Revolution took place, discrimination against non-Muslims became official government policy. You could and were cancelled for being opposed to government policy, and speaking your mind could land you in jail or dead.

My parents saw the writing on the wall, and decided it was time to leave the only home we had ever known, to go live in a country where our religion and our ethnic background would not be held against us.

I was 13 years old at the time, and none of this was obvious to me. I knew was that we were leaving all our home and our friends and family behind, and I hated it. A 13-year old is old enough to make his family's life unpleasant if he chose to, and I alternated between being the good son and the bratty son.

But over time, I came to appreciate the freedoms that we had in Canada, and I fell in love with my new adopted country. I could go out and tell my friends, publicly, that I couldn't stand the Prime Minister — heck, I could even call him dirty names — and I was in no danger of being picked up by the secret police and hauled off to jail. Back home, my parents had to be eternally vigilant to make sure that my brothers and I kept our mouths shut about our country's rulers, lest the secret police show up in the middle of the night and haul us all away to Evin Prison.

If you've never heard of that prison, it's one of the most notorious jails for political prisoners on earth. People imprisoned there, who have been lucky enough to get out, say that it's hell on earth. It's scorching hot in the summer, and numbingly cold in the winter. The guards treat prisoners brutally, and torture is commonplace. Lots of prisoners don't make it out alive, and these are people who have NOT been sentenced to death.

Experiencing how free we were in Canada made me fall in love with it. Women can walk around here without having to cover themselves with a *chador*, a garment that covers them from head to toe, lest the religious police harass or beat them publicly for "shameless" behavior. You can be openly gay here, and not have to worry about hiding in "the closet," because openly gay men and women back home are sentenced to death and thrown off tall buildings to their death. And you didn't need to be the 'right" color, religion, or ethnic background to apply to schools, or for jobs.

All of that was amazing to me. I devoured books about freedom, and her champions. I came to see that freedom wasn't free, and that good men and women had fought, bled and died so that we, today, could enjoy our awesome blessings. At age 20, I was introduced by a friend to the world of Ayn Rand, and her philosophy of Objectivism appealed to the idealist within me. And then, like so many young men and women my age, I was mesmerized by Ronald Reagan and Margaret Thatcher, and their moral clarity in the battle versus Godless communism during the Cold War. I devoured all their speeches, and vowed to be a warrior for freedom just like them.

But then, in large part thanks to Reagan and Thatcher, as well as Pope John Paul II, the West won the Cold War.

It didn't seem as urgent, or necessary, to be a warrior for freedom.

And so, I got into business, working for a large telecom concern, and enjoyed the freedom granted to me to engage in the pursuit of happiness. But I still felt the fire, the zeal to stand up for freedom whenever and wherever I could.

My passion to uphold freedom was just like that of an ex-smoker to eradicate smoking. To me, freedom, free expression, and free enterprise are sacred gifts from God, that every man and woman on earth deserves to have and enjoy the blessings that they offer.

I still believed that the battle for freedom had been won, and that there was no need to engage in it, certainly not as seriously as I did during the Cold War.

**But now I see that that I was wrong.**

Ronald Reagan once said that *"Freedom is never more than one generation away from extinction. We didn't pass it to our children in the bloodstream. It must be fought for, protected, and handed on for them to do the same, or one day we will spend our sunset years telling our children and our children's children what it was once like in the United States where men were free."*

Boy, was he ever right.

There are forces within the West that are actively fighting to suppress freedom for ALL OF US. The first thing they did was frontally attack free speech through political correctness and speech codes on college campuses.

Those of us who love freedom were not unduly alarmed. After all, college isn't "real life."

But soon, this way of thinking spread to all public schools, Hollywood, social media, sports and the rest of society. Not to mention mainstream media 24/7/365.

The Democrat Party, which has flirted with totalitarianism throughout its existence, is now firmly in the grips of the freedom grabbers. In the 1800s, and up until the 1960s, the Democrats were an overtly racist party, standing for white supremacy and the oppression of blacks and other minorities.

But in the '60s, a shrewd and amoral man had them change tactics. Lyndon Johnson, a racist man to his core, realized that overt racism was the path to electoral doom for the Democrats. So, he collaborated with the Republican Party and passed Civil Rights and Voting Rights legislation. He, in effect, rebranded the Democrat Party.

Now, the Democrats came across as 'caring." But in reality, they were still the same racists they had always been. They implemented polices like welfare that ended up breaking up the black family and making black men irrelevant in the rearing of their children. Their entire policy was based on gaslighting voters into believing that Republicans — you know, the party created *SPECIFICALLY* to abolish racism — were the real racists. Democrat policies were meant to keep blacks dependent on government handouts, and Democrat politicians and their supporters kept screaming "racist" at any attempt to make blacks more self-sufficient and less dependent on government.

The Republicans, being less amoral and cunning than the Democrats, did not fight back against these scurrilous charges, and instead weakly protested that they were not racist.

The media, social media (Silicon Valley), academia, union bosses, and Hollywood have all backed up the Democrat narrative, and until the election of President Donald J. Trump, no Republican seriously contested the Democrats' hold on the black vote.

Trump actively courted black voters in speeches, with policies like The First Step Act, and with a bold "Contract with Black America," proclaiming that he intended to create $500 billion in black wealth.

The Dems have fought hard, gaslighting us all with their usual racist trope, and desperately seeking to hide their own true racism.

But it's become harder and harder for them to do that. For one, Kamala Harris is on record calling Biden's opposition to school busing "racist." And Biden himself was friends with actual segregationists throughout the '70s and '80s, and has made questionable offensive statement after statement, including saying "the n-word" during a speech in 2021.

So, now Democrats have enlisted the gigantic multi-national corporations (most publicly traded) in a last desperate attempt to shut down free speech and destroy the ability of freedom-loving people to make their voices heard.

Never in a million years did I expect business leaders to fight against the very freedom that gave them the greatest possible life on earth. But there are executives at the top levels of companies today that do not stand for freedom, free expression, and free enterprise. They stand for the opposite. And they are quite vocal about it.

One of the battles they are choosing to fight is a battle against free and secure elections. They are vociferously opposed to things like voting in-person, voter ID, and restricting the dangerous scheme known as "mail-in voting."

To me, as someone who first-hand saw a fraudulent election in my country of origin, this is messed up. I consider any white leftist telling me (as a light brown Middle Eastern man) that I am too ignorant to get ID to vote, to be a condescending racist jerk!

As an immigrant, I am telling you that the ONLY way to have an honest election is with in-person voting, with voter ID. The ONLY time you should be allowed to do mail-in voting is if you are out of state or the country, and can prove that you can't vote in-person. Otherwise, it's too easy to cheat and subvert the process. In Europe, mail-in voting is BANNED because it is widely recognized to be an invitation to cheat!

I ask these companies: why do you insist that we show you ID to prove our identity when we do business with you, and yet are opposed to having us show ID to vote? If I wish to board a plane, I have to show a passport, or a driver's license. If I wish to open a bank account, I need ID. If I wish to write a check to pay for groceries, I need ID. If I want welfare, or food stamps, or free healthcare from government, I must show valid ID.

Another issue is auditing election results in battle-ground states. I am not going to claim I know one way or another that these elections were free and fair or not. But back home, I saw first-hand how "the swamp" rigged an election. My dad walked into a polling place with his ballot. A man in military uniform, carrying an assault rifle pointed it at him and growled "Give me that!" he snatched the ballot form my dad's hands, marked it, and put it in the ballot box. He stared at my dad and growled "You can go now."

My dad walked out of that polling place, humiliated and angry. That's when he said to me "Son, I'm going take you and the family to place where your vote counts and no one can rig an election and take your voice away."

He and I talked about it lots of times. He told me about other ways the vote was rigged in our country. The folks counting were from one party (think about government workers here in the USA—they're almost 100% Democrats). The other party's observers were kicked out of the room (think Pennsylvania, Georgia, Arizona). In Atlanta, there was a water-main break, and everyone was kicked out of the polling place. In Detroit, the vote counters blacked out the windows with pizza boxes so no GOP observers could see in. In Philadelphia, GOP poll observers were refused entry to the vote counting room, even with a court order from a judge in their hands. Don't forget those same government vote counters, who claimed that hundreds of thousands of new ballots came in, almost 100% for the government candidate (Biden) in places like Michigan, Pennsylvania, Georgia, and Wisconsin. This all reminds me of voting in my home country of Iran.

For me, this shows that there were enough irregularities in the vote in Arizona, Georgia, Michigan, Wisconsin, Nevada, and Pennsylvania that having an honest audit makes sense. If these elections were mostly fair, then an audit will just confirm it. Of course, Democrats lose their minds at the mere mention of a forensic audit. Something must be scaring them to death.

But these "woke" companies are selling out (out of fear and intimidation) to the left because they are more scared of BLM, antifa and crazed liberal activists, than they are of the salt-of-the-earth people who vote Republican.

Why?

Because the left is loud and engages in boycotts.

The reason why we wrote this book is to encourage the Silent Majority (the normal people) who are not crazy, totalitarian leftists, socialists or communist revolutionaries — to push back.

Any company that does not represent your values and caves to the leftist mob must be held to account by its customers, through protesting, boycotts, and LEAVING as a customer forever.

It's time for the rest of us to make these companies more scared of offending us, than the crazy lefties and commies.

How?

One, by taking our money elsewhere. Two, by calling, and emailing these companies to let them know we are not amused, they are attacking our core shared values of morality, Judeo-Christian morality, capitalism, patriotism and American exceptionalism. Three, letting them know with these calls sand emails that there will be very real financial consequences for their behavior. Finally, four, calling and emailing our elected representatives and demanding that they remove ALL incentives, government contracts and corporate welfare giveaways to these woke corporations.

Governor Ron DeSantis has led the way on this. He just signed a bill attacking woke big tech firms who cancel and censor conservatives and patriots. Other states like Texas are about to follow. This is a good first step, but we need way more.

I call all freedom-loving political leaders in states, counties and cities that have provided tax and other benefits to these corporations to review their behavior, and withdraw all incentives from companies that kowtow to the leftist mob and attack normal, regular people and politicians. Just as Georgia took away incentives from Delta when Delta supported the removal of the Baseball All Star game from Atlanta. It's time to fight fire with fire.

We are free men and women. We need to stop spending money and rewarding companies that spit in our face. These companies must be taught a lesson.

It's time for us to band together, and to cancel any corporation that doesn't stay out of the political and culture wars.

That's why Wayne and I wrote this book.

**Nicky Billou, July 2021**

# CHAPTER 11

# HOW TO GET THE WOKE CEOs ATTENTION, FAST

Now we have given you a list of 100+ of the most egregiously woke corporations, along with their contact phone numbers and email addresses. But you know what's going to happen. As soon as some of the CEOs of these corporations get called or emailed, they're likely going to change their contact phone numbers and email addresses to avoid the avalanche of irate actual customers that they're going to have contacting them (about 80 million if all goes well).

That's easy for them to do, and they will do it.

What's harder for them to do, and they won't do, is to abandon their social media presence.

And frankly, that's where the woke left mob has been attacking these corporations and getting them to cave to their demands. The left is loud, smart and vicious. Two can play at that game.

Jesse Waters, our 2nd favorite conservative talk show host (the co-author of this book WAR will always be #1 in our hearts) has a very perceptive take on this.

The angry people that have been complaining to corporations have been around for a long time. The same 100 to 200 people and their ilk have been writing letters and making phone calls to companies since at least the 1960s. The reason they were ineffective in the past is that no CEO ever saw their complaints. They had gatekeepers whose job was to insulate the boss from the angry people. The angry letters and phone calls never reached the top.

As a result, the complaints of the angry customers went nowhere. Even the ones who had every right to be angry were ignored.

**The rise of social media changed all that.**

Now, the hate-filled politically-correct cranks, crackpots and snowflakes (liberals offended by everything) could get their messages in front of the CEO because their angry tirades were out there for anyone to see. Complaints about a corporation and its practices have now become very public, and there is no way to insulate the CEO from them. Even if the old-fashioned gatekeepers could keep these social media posts and videos away from the CEO, their family and friends would tell them about all the nasty things that are being written about them and their company on social media. And that would embarrass them in a very real and personal way.

And most of these companies have made the HUGE mistake of hiring a social media manger. This is a job that never existed prior to 2010. But now many companies deem it essential. And the person filling the role is invariably a wonkish individual, usually young, eager, and wrong about everything that matters in life and business. And what they do, because they have been brainwashed into believing this woke B.S., is to echo the complainers' message, and convince their CEOs that these cranks are representative of their customer base, and unless they change their company policies to conform with their customers demands, the company is doomed!

CEOs, not being very tech or social media savvy, have bought this line of baloney *en masse*. And thus, "cancel culture" was born. All of these woke corporations are responding to an online mob. They are not really woke. They don't really believe in much of anything, expect the almighty dollar.

Never mind that most of these complainers are NOT customers of these companies; they never have been, and never will be. Never mind that they have no real ability to hurt these companies bottom line because they are (a) tiny in number and (b) let me repeat, not actually customers!

One other reality. Liberals don't make the money. Conservatives do. So even if the split is 50/50, no matter. The 50% who are conservative make up 60% to 70% of the sales revenues. So, our opinions matter much more.

That is the craziness of it all! To listen to the left mob will destroy any business. They are only the LOUD minority. We (conservatives, Christians, capitalists) are the Silent Majority. We buy your products. We spend the big bucks. We are the ones who actually matter!

It's time for those of us who love America and all that she stands for to beat the woke mob at its own game!

All of these CEOs and companies will respond if the freedom lovers among us, those of us who are actually customers of these corporations: (A) vote with our dollars and (B) use social media to let our displeasure at their craven hypocrisy and caving to the woke cranks, be felt.

The woke mob usually number about 100 or 200 people, going after these companies in a rush of anger and vitriol through social media. What if we had their accounts flooded with 100,000 or 200,000 patriots posting about their displeasure at their woke (ie dumb, clueless, anti-American, anti-freedom, anti-capitalist) policies and assault on the very foundation of freedom that makes America, America?

## WE COULD REALLY CHANGE THE DIRECTION OF AMERICA.

Each of these companies on the list has a Facebook, Twitter, and Instagram account. They are easy to find. Just go onto Instagram, Twitter, and Facebook and type in their company name. Then post on their pages, and tell them that you're an actual customer and you don't appreciate them bringing leftist politics into business, and you're going to vote with your dollars and leave. And take some of your friends who you know feel the same way as you, and get them to also post their displeasure and threaten to leave.

**Here are some tips:**

One, always be respectful and civil. Use polite language. No swearing. No nastiness. Just direct, straight talk, and direct straight action by taking your business elsewhere. Let the left come from hate. You come from God, faith, family and patriotism.

Two, get your friends to do the same.

Three, pray for them to listen and change direction.

Four, find companies that are not woke and take your business there.

It's really that simple. Heck, we're gonna make it even easier for you to find their social media accounts. We are going to give you a list of 100+ of these companies, along with hyperlinks to their Twitter, Facebook, and Instagram accounts. Go for it.

Remember,

Be civil.
Come from love.
Be direct.
**Vote with your dollars.**

God bless,

Wayne Allyn Root & Nicky Billou

# American Woke Company Boycott List

| Company Name | Headquarters/ Corporate Mailing Address in USA | Contact Number | Chairman of the Board | Chairman's Email | CEO | CEO's Email | Service / Product |
|---|---|---|---|---|---|---|---|
| Abercrombie & Fitch, Co. | 6301 Fitch Path, New Albany, OH 43054 | 614-283-6500 | Arthur Martinez N/A (VP Larry Grischow) | larry_grischow@ abercrombie.com | Fran Horowitz | Only VP Justin Brannon email avail justin_lee_brannon@yahoo.com | Authentic American Clothing |
| Accenture | 161 N Clark St, Chicago, IL, 60601-3362 | 312-693-0161 | Julie Sweet | julie.sweet@accenture.com | Julie Sweet | julie.sweet@ accenture.com | Online services technology consultants, telemarketing services, management consulting services |
| Adidas | 5055 N Greeley Avenue Portland, OR 97217 | 800-982-9337 | Thomas Rabe | investor.relations@ adidas.com | Zion Armstrong | zion.armstrong@ adidas.com | Athletic Wear and Sports Shoes |
| Adobe Inc. | 345 Park Ave, San Jose, CA 95110-2704 | 408-536-6000 | Shantanu Narayen | shantanu.narayen@ adobe.com | Shantanu Narayen | shantanu.narayen@adobe.com | Computer Software & Media |
| Airbnb | 888 Brannan St. San Francisco, CA, 94103-4928 | 415-510-4027 | Brian Chesky | brian.chesky@airbnb.com | Brian Chesky | brian.chesky@ airbnb.com | Travel Agencies & Services |
| Alphabet Inc. | 1600 Amphitheatre Parkway, Mountain View, California 94043 | 650-253-0000 | John L. Hennessy | N/A | Sundar Pichai | sunda@gmail.com | American multinational conglomerate company |
| AMC Theatres | 11500 Ash St, Leawood, KS, 66211-7804 | 913-213-2000 | Lin Zhang | N/A | General Manager - Amanda Avery | amanda.r.avery@ gmail.com | Movie Theatres & Media |

| Company | Address | Phone | Contact | Email | Contact | Email | Description |
|---|---|---|---|---|---|---|---|
| Apple Inc. | 1 Apple Park Way, Cupertino, CA, 95014-0642 | 408-996-1010 | Arthur D. Levinson | levinson@apple.com | Tim Cook | tcook@apple.com | Technology Company |
| Asurion Corporation | 648 Grassmere Park, Suite 300, Nashville, TN 37211 | 615-837-3000 | Kevin Taweel | ktaweel@asurion.com | Bret Comolli | bret_comolli@asurion.com | Property, Casualty Insurance Carriers |
| AT&T | 208 S Akard St, Dallas, TX, 75202-4206 | 210-821-4105 | N/A | N/A | John T. Stankey | john.stankey@att.com | Wireless Communication Services & Media |
| Bain & Company | 131 Dartmouth Street Boston, MA 02116 | 617-572-2000 | Orit Gadiesh | N/A | Manny Maceda | Manny.Maceda@bain.com | Global consultancy that helps the world's most ambitious change-makers define the future |
| Bank of America | 100 North Tryon Street, Charlotte, NC 28255 | 844-373-7028 | Brian Thomas Moynihan | brian.moynihan@bankofamerica.com | Brian Thomas Moynihan | brian.moynihan@bankofamerica.com | Financial |
| Bed, Bath & Beyond | 650 Liberty Ave, Union, NJ 07083 | 908-688-0888 | Mark J Tritton | mark.tritton@bedbath.com | Mark J. Tritton | mark.tritton@bedbath.com | Home Furnishing Stores, Bedding, Linens, Gifts etc. |
| Belk | 2801 West Tyvola Road, Charlotte, NC 28217-4500 | 704-357-1000 | Stefan Kaluzny | N/A | Lisa M. Harper | lharpermail@aol.com | A department store chain and online store offering apparel, shoes, accessories, cosmetics, home furnishings and wedding registry |
| Ben & Jerry Ice Cream | 30 Community Dr #1. South Burlington, VT 05403 | 802-846-1500 | Jennifer Henderson | jennifer.henderson@benjerry.com | Matthew McCarthy | mattrmc@gmail.com | Ice Cream |
| Berkshire Hathaway | 3555 Farnam Street Omaha, NE 68131 | 402-346-1400 | Warren Buffett | berkshire@berkshirehathaway.com | Warren Buffett | berkshire@berkshirehathaway.com | American multinational conglomerate company |
| Best Buy | 7601 Penn Avenue, South Richfield, MN 55423 | 612-291-1000 | J. Patrick Doyle | N/A | Corie Barry | corry.barry@bestbuy.com | Consumer electronics retailer |

| Company | Address | Phone | Chairman | Email | CEO | CEO Email | Description |
|---|---|---|---|---|---|---|---|
| Bing (Owned & Operated By Microsoft) | One Microsoft Way, Redmond, WA 98052 | 425-882-8080 | John W. Thompson | johnw@microsoft.com | Steve Ballmer | sballmer@microsoft.com | Microsoft Search Engine |
| BMC Software | 2103 Citywest Blvd Suite 2100 Houston, TX 77042-2857 | 713-918-8800 | Bob Beauchamp | N/A | Ayman Sayed | ayman_sayed@bmc.com | Helps customers run and reinvent their businesses with open, scalable, and modular solutions to complex IT problems |
| Boston Consulting Group | 200 Pier 4 Blvd Boston, MA 02210 | 617-973-1200 | Hans-Paul Burkner | Buerkner.Hans-Paul@bcg.com | Rich Lesser | rich@consulting.ca | Management Consulting Company |
| Calvin Klein (Owned by PVH Corp.) | 205 W 39th St, New York, NY 10018 | 212-719-2600 | Manny Chirico (PVH) | emanuelchirico@pvh.com | Cheryl Abel-Hodges | cherylabel-hodges@ck.com | Fashion Company |
| Capital One | 1680 Capital One Dr, McLean, VA 22102-3407 | 703-720-1000 | Richard Fairbank | Richard.Fairbank@capitalone.com | Richard Fairbank | Richard.Fairbank@capitalone.com | Issuers of Visa and MasterCard credit cards in the US. |
| Chewy Inc. | 1855 Griffin Road, Dania Beach, FL 33004 | 800-672-4399 | Raymond Svider | Investor Relations - ir@chewy.com | Sumit Singh | N/A | Pet & Pet Food Supplies |
| Chipotle | 610 Newport Center Dr #1300, Newport Beach, CA 92660 | 303-595-4000 | Brian Niccol | bniccol@chipotle.com | Brian Niccol | bniccol@chipotle.com | Mexican Restauraunt |
| Cisco Systems | 170 W Tasman Dr, San Jose, CA, 95134-1706 | 408-526-4000 | Chuck Robbins | crobbins@cisco.com | Chuck Robbins | crobbins@cisco.com | Data conversion equipment, media-to-media: computer, online services technology consultant |
| Citigroup | 388 Greenwich St, New York, NY 10013 | 212-559-1000 | John C. Dugan | N/A | Jane Fraser | jane.fraser@citigroup.com | Financial services firms |

| Company | Address | Phone | Chairman & President | Email | Senior VP | Email | Description |
|---|---|---|---|---|---|---|---|
| CNN | 190 Marietta St NW, Atlanta, GA, 30303-2762 | 404-878-2276 | Jeff Zucker (Chairman & President) | N/A | Senior VP Robyn Peterson | robert.peterson@cnn.com | Television Broadcasting & Media |
| Coca Cola | 1 Coca Cola Plz NW, Atlanta, GA 30312 | 404-676-2121 | Jame Quincey | jquincey@coca-cola.com | Jame Quincey | jquincey@coca-cola.com | Food Manufacturing, Concentrates, Drinks, Syrups |
| Colony Brands Inc. | 1112 7TH Ave, Monroe, WI, 53566-1364 | 608-328-8400 | Raymond Kubly Junior | raymondk@colonybrands.com | John Baumann | johnb@colonybrands.com | Internet & Mail Order Retail |
| Comcast Corporation | 1701 John F Kennedy Blvd, Philadelphia, PA 19103, | 215-583-8078 | Brian L. Roberts | brian_roberts@comcast.com | Brian L. Roberts | brian_roberts@comcast.com | TV Broadcast & Cable Networks Media |
| Costco | 999 Lake Drive Issaquah, WA 98027 | 425-313-8103 | Hamilton E. James | N/A | Craig Jelinek | cjelinek@costco.com | Multinational corporation which operates a chain of membership-only big-box retail stores |
| Cover Girl - Owned by Coty | 11050 York Rd, Cockeysville, MD 21030 | 410-785-7300 | Peter Harf (Coty Chairman) | peter_harf@cotyinc.com | Sue Nabi (Coty CEO) | synlumiere@gmail.com | Fashion/Make-up Retail Company |
| Delta Airlines Inc. | 1030 Delta Blvd, Atlanta, GA, 30354-1989 | 404-715-2600 | Frank Blake | frank.blake@delta.com | Edward H. Bastian | edward.bastian@delta.com | Airline Service |
| Diacom Corporation | 5 Howe Dr. Amherst, NH, 03031-2315 | 603-880-1900 | N/A | Direct email to: marka@diacom.com - Controller | Scott Rafferty | scottr@diacom.com | Plastic & Rubber Product Manufacturing |
| Dick Sporting | 345 Court Street Coraopolis, PA 15108 | 724-273-3400 | Edward Stack | edward.stack@dickssportinggoods.com | Edward Stack | edward.stack@dickssportinggoods.com | Retail Company |
| Disney | 500 S. Buena Vista Street Burbank, CA 91521 | 818-560-1000 | Robert Igar | robert.a.iger@disney.com | Bob Chapek | chapek@disney.com | Entertainment |

| Company | Address | Phone | Name | Email | Name | Email | Description |
|---|---|---|---|---|---|---|---|
| Dollar General Corporation | 100 Mission RDG, Goodlettsville, TN, 37072-2171 | 615-855-4000 | Michael Calbert | mcalbert@dollargeneral.com | Todd J. Vasos | tvasos@dollargeneral.com | Discount Department Stores |
| Dow Chemical Company | 47 Building Midland, Michigan 48667 | 989-636-1000 | Jim Fitterling | jrfitter@yahoo.com | Howard Ungerleider | hungerleider@dow.com | Plastic, Resin & Synthetic Fiber manufacturing |
| Estee Lauder Companies | 767 Fifth Avenue, 40th Floor, New York, NY 10153 | 212-572-4200 | William P. Lauder | wlauder@estee.com | Fabrizio Freda N/A (VP Beth Guastella Email) | bethgnyc@gmail.com | Skin care, fragrances and make-up products |
| Etsy | 117 Adams Street, Brooklyn, NY 11201 | 718-880-3660 | Fred Wilson | N/A | Josh Silverman | jsilverman@gmail.com | e-commerce website focused on handmade or vintage items and craft supplies |
| Expedia Group | 1111 Expedia Group Way West Seattle, WA 98119 | 877-227-7481 | Barry Diller | bdiller@expediagroup.com | Peter M. Kern | pkern@expediagroup.com | Travel Agencies and Services |
| Facebook | 1 Hacker Way, Menlo Park, CA 94025 | 650-308-7300 | Mark Zuckerburg | zuckerburg@fb.com | Mark Zuckerburg | zuckerburg@fb.com | Social Media |
| Gap Inc. | 2 Folsom Street, San Francisco, CA 94105 | 650-952-4400 | Robert J. Fisher | bobbi_fisher@gap.com | Sonia Syngal | sonia.syngal@sbcglobal.net | Worldwide clothing and accessory retailer |
| General Motors, | 300 Renaissance Center Detroit, MI 48243 | 313-667-1500 | Mary Barra | mary.barra@gm.com | Mary Barra | mary.barra@gm.com | Vehicle Manufacturer |
| Girl Scouts | 420 Fifth Avenue at 37th Street – Ground Floor | N/A | N/A | N/A | Judith Batty | jbatty@girlscouts.org | A youth organization for girls in the United States and American girls living abroad |
| Go Daddy | 14455 N Hayden Rd Suite 219, Scottsdale AZ 85260-6993 | 480-505-8877 | Scott W Wagner | swagner@godaddy.com | Aman Bhutani | N/A | Information Technology |

| Company | Address | Phone | Name | Email | Name | Email | Description |
|---|---|---|---|---|---|---|---|
| Goldman Sachs | 200 West Street New York, NY 10282 | 212-902-1000 | David M. Solomon | davidsol145@gmail.com | David M. Solomon | davidsol145@gmail.com | Investment Banking Company |
| Goodyear | 200 Innovation Way, Akron, OH 44316 | 330-796-2121 | Richard J. Kramer | Rich_Kramer@goodyear.com | Richard J. Kramer | Rich_Kramer@goodyear.com | Tire & Rubber Company |
| Google | 1600 Amphitheatre Parkway, Moutain View, CA 94043 | 650-253-0000 | John Hennessy | hennessy@stanford.edu | Thomas Kurian | tkurian@google.com | Information Technology Services |
| Groupon, Inc. | 600 W Chicago Ave Suite 400, Chicago, IL 60654-2067 | 312-334-1579 | Erin Lefkofsky | N/A | Aaron Cooper | acooper@groupon.com | Advertising Agency - earns commissions by selling goods or services on behalf of third-party merchants |
| GrubHub | 111 West Washington Street Suite 2100 Chicago, IL 60602 | 800-905-9332 | Brian McAndrews | N/A | Matt Maloney | matt@grubhub.com | Online Food Ordering Service |
| H & M | 110 Fifth Avenue, 11th Floor, New York, NY 10011 | 212-564-9922 | Stefan Persson | stefan@nortex.se | Helena Helmersson | helena.lundberg@hotmail.com | Clothing retail company |
| Harrys, Inc. | 75 Varick St, New York, NY 10013 | 888-212-6855 | N/A | N/A | Jeffrey Raider (Co-Founder & Co-CEO) | Jeffrey.Raider@gmail.com | Manufactures and sells shaving equipment and men's personal care products via online and retail channels |
| HP | 20555 State Highway 249, Houston, TX 77070 | 281-370-0670 | Chip Bergh | N/A | Enrique Lores | enrique.lores@hp.com | Printers, desktops, laptops, servers, storage, enterprise solutions and more |
| Hyundai Motor Company USA | 10550 Talbert Avenue, Fountain Valley, CA 92708-0850 | 714-965-3000 | Euisun Chung | N/A | Jose Munoz | jmunoz@hmausa.com | Automotive manufacturer |

| Company | Address | Phone | Name | Email | Name | Email | Description |
|---|---|---|---|---|---|---|---|
| IBM | 1 New Orchard Rd, Suite 1 Armonk, NY 10504-1722 | 914-499-1900 | Arvind Krishna | akrishna@ibm.com | N/A | N/A | Personal Computer Manufacturing |
| Ikea | 420 Allen Wood Road, Conshohocken, PA 19428 | 610-834-0180 | Anders Dahlvig | N/A | Javier Quiñones | jquinonesc9@gmail.com | Furnishing and Home Furnishings |
| Instagram | 1 Hacker Way, Menlo Park, CA 94025 | 650-543-4800 | Kevin Systrom | kevins@instagram.com | Adam Mosseri | Adam@fb.com | Social Media |
| Intel | 2200 Mission College Blvd. Santa Clara, CA 95054-1549 | 408-765-8080 | Dr. Omar Ishrak | Omar.Isharak@intel.com | Patrick P. Gelsinger | patrick.gelsinger@intel.com | Computer Products ie microprocessors |
| JC Penney | 6501 Legacy Dr,, Plano, TX 75024 | 972-431-1000 | Ron Tysoe | tysoer@jcpenney.com | Jill Soltau | soltauj@natividad.com | Retail sector |
| Jet Blue | 27-01 Queens Plaza, North, Long Island City, NY 11101 | 718-286-7900 | Joel Peterson N/A (VP Doug McGraw) | doug.mcgraw@jetblue.com | Robin Hayes | robin.hayes@jetblue.com | American low cost airline |
| Kelloggs | 1 Kellogg Sq, Battle Creek, MI, 49017-3534 | 731-423-7100 | James M. Jenness | N/A | Steve Cahillane | steve@kellogg.com | Cookie & Cracker Manufacturing Industry |
| Kohl's Corportion | N56 W17000 Ridgewood Drive, Menomonee Falls, WI 53051 | 262-703-7000 | Frank V. Sica | frank.sica@kohls.com | Michelle Gass | michelle.gass@gmail.com | Department Store |
| L Brand | Three Limited Parkway Columbus, OH 43230 | 614-415-7000 | Andrew Meslow | andrew.meslow@bathandbodyworks.com (ameslow@lb.com) | Andrew Meslow (also CEO of Bath & Body) | andrew.meslow@bathandbodyworks.com | Retail Company |
| LinkedIn | 1000 West Maude Avenue, Sunnyvale, CA 94085 | 855-655-5653 | Kathleen Taylor | ktaylor@linkedin.com | Ryan Roslansky | rroslansky@linkedin.com | On-line professional network database |

| Company | Address | Phone | Name | Email | Name | Email | Description |
|---|---|---|---|---|---|---|---|
| L'oreal USA | 10 Hudson Yards, 347 10th Ave, New York, NY 10001 | 212-818-1500 | Jean-Paul Agon | THERET@loreal.com | Jean-Paul Agon | THERET@loreal.com | Cosmetic, Beauty Supply & Perfume Store |
| Lyft | 185 Berry St. San Francisco, CA 94107-5705 | 855-865-9953 | Sean Aggarwal | sean@lyft.com | John Zimmer - President | john@lyft.com | Mobile App, Hired Drivers, Delivery |
| Macy's | 151 West 34th Street, New York, NY 10001 | 212-494-3000 | Jeff Gennette | Jeff.gennette@macys.com | Jeff Gennette | Jeff.gennette@macys.com | Fashion retailers and department stores |
| Mailchimp | 675 Ponce De Leon Avenue, Northeast, Suite 5000, Atlanta, GA 30308 | 678-999-0141 | N/A | N/A | Ben Chestnut | ben@rocketsciencegroup.com | Marketing automation platform and email marketing service |
| Major League Baseball (MLB) | 75 9th Ave, New York, NY 10011 | 212-485-3444 | N/A | N/A | Rob McGlarry | rob.mcglarry@mlb.com | Baseball League |
| Marvel | 135 W 50th St, New York, NY 10020 | 212-576-4000 | Issac Perlmutter | N/A | Dan Buckley (President) | dbuckley@marvel.com | Publishing Company |
| Mastercard | 2000 Purchase St, Purchase, NY 10577 | 914-249-2000 | Ajay Banga | ajay_banga@mastercard.com | Michael Miebach | mmiebach@mastercard.com | Financial Services Company |
| Mattress Firm Bedquarters | 10201 S Main St, Houston, TX 77025 | 866-942-3551 | N/A | N/A | John Eck | John.Eck@mfrm.com | Matress Store |
| McDonalds Corporation | 110 North Carpenter Street, One McDonald's Plaza, Chicago, IL 60607 | 630-623-3000 | Enrique Hernandez Jr. | N/A | Chris Kempczinski | ckempczinski@gmail.com | Fast food and quick service restaurants |
| Merck | 2000 Galloping Hill Road, Kenilworth, NJ 07033 | 908-740-4000 | Kevin Frazier until Jun 20/21 Retires | kevin.frazier@merck.com | Kevin Frazier until Jun 20/21 Retires | kevin.frazier@merck.com | Pharmaceutical company |

| Company | Address | Phone | Contact | Email | Contact 2 | Email 2 | Business |
|---|---|---|---|---|---|---|---|
| Microsoft Corporation | 1 Microsoft Way, Redmond, WA 98052-8300 | 425-882-8080 | John W Thompson | johnw@microsoft.com | Satya Nadella | satyan@microsoft.com | Computer Software & Media |
| Mondelez International | 100 Deforest Avenue, East Hanover, NJ 07936 | 855-535-5648 | Dirk Van De Put | dirk-vandeput@hotmail.com | Dirk Van De Put | dirk-vandeput@hotmail.com | Confectionery, food, holding and beverage and snack food company |
| National Football League | 345 Park Avenue, New York, NY 10154 | 330-962-7272 | Charlotte Jones Anderson | canderson@dallascowboys.net | Roger Goodell | Roger.goodell@NFL.com | Profession Football League |
| NBA | 645 5th Avenue, New York City, New York, 10022 | 212-407-8000 | Shareef Abdur-Rahim (President NBA Development League) | shareef924@gmail.com | Byron Spruell (President of League Operations) | bspruell@nba.com | Basketball League |
| Netflix, Inc. | 100 Winchester Cir, Los Gatos, CA, 95032-1815 | 408-540-3700 | Reed Hastings | reed.hastings@netflix.com | N/A | N/A | Internet Streaming Company Distributing Videos |
| New York Times | 620 Eighth Avenue, New York, NY 10018 | 800-698-4637 | Arthur Gregg Agsulzberger | agsulzberger@nytimes.com | Meredith Kopit Levien | mlevien@nytimes.com | Newspaper |
| Next Door | 875 Stevenson Street Suite 700 San Francisco, CA 94103 | 415-569-7971 | John Hope Bryant | N/A | Sarah Friar | sarahf@nextdoor.com | Social Media Service |
| Nike | One Bowerman Dr, Beaverton, OR 97005 | 503-671-6453 | Philip H. Knight | philip@nike.co.kr | John Donohue | john.donohue@nike.com | Footwear Manufacturing |
| Nordstrom | 1700 7th Ave. Ste. 1500, Seattle, WA 98101 | 877-746-6228 | Brad Smith | brad.smith@nordstrom.com | Erik B. Nordstrom | erik.nordstrom@nordstrom.com | Luxury department store chain |
| Nvidia Corporation | 2788 San Tomas Expy, Santa Clara, CA, 95051-0952 | 408-486-2000 | N/A | N/A | Jen-Hsun Huang | jensenhuang@nvidia.com | Semiconductor & Other Electronic Component Manufacturing |

| Company | Address | Phone | Contact | Email | Name | Email | Description |
|---|---|---|---|---|---|---|---|
| Office Depot | 6600 N Military Trl, Boca Raton, FL 33496-2434 | 561-438-4800 | Stephen A Odland | N/A | Gerry Smith | Gerry.Smith@officedepot.com | Paper & Pen Supplies |
| P&G | One Procter & Gamble Plaza, Cincinnati, OH 45201 | 513-983-1100 | David S. Taylor | taylor.da@pg.com | David S. Taylor | taylor.da@pg.com | Consumer Goods |
| Patagonia | 259 West Santa Clara Street, Ventura, CA 93001 | 805-643-8616 | N/A | N/A | Ryan Gellert | gellertryan@gmail.com | Outdoor clothing and gear |
| Pepsico, Inc. | 700 Anderson Hill Road, Purchase, NY 10577 | 914-253-2000 | Ramon Laguarta | Ramon.Laguarta@pepsico.com | Ramon Laguarta | Ramon.Laguarta@pepsico.com | An American multinational food, snack, and beverage corporation |
| Pinterest | 651 Brannan St, San Francisco, CA 94107 | 415-762-7100 | Ben Silbermann | bensilbermann@gmail.com | Ben Silbermann | bensilbermann@gmail.com | Social Media Service |
| Progressive Corp. | 6300 Wilson Mills Rd, Mayfield, OH 44143 | 440-575-5119 | Peter B. Louis | peter_louis@progressive.com | Tricia Griffith | tricia_griffith@progressive.com | Insurance Corporation |
| Reddit | 420 Taylor Street, San Francisco, CA 94102 | 424-234-9948 | Ryan Cohen | ryandcohen@gmail.com | Steve Huffman | steven@reddit.com | A social news aggregation, web content rating, and discussion website |
| Salesforce | Tower 415 Mission Street, 3rd Floor San Francisco, CA 94105 | 415-901-7000 | Marc Benioff | ceo@salesforce.com | Marc Benioff | ceo@salesforce.com | Cloud based software company |
| Sephora | 525 Market St FL 32, San Francisco, CA 94105-2740 | 415-284-3300 | N/A | N/A | Jean-André Rougeot | ExternalComms@sephora.com (only email avail) | Cosmetics, Beauty Supply & Perfume Stores Retail Sector |
| Simon & Shuster | 1230 Avenue of the Americas, New York, NY, 10020. | 508-427-7100 | Jonathan Karp | jonathan.karp@simonandschuster.com | Jonathan Karp | jonathan.karp@simonandschuster.com | American publishing company and a subsidiary of ViacomCBS |

| Company | Address | Phone | Contact | Email | Contact | Email | Description |
|---|---|---|---|---|---|---|---|
| Snap Chat | 2772 Donald Douglas, Loop North Santa Monica, CA 90405 | 310-399-3339 | Michael Lynton | michael.lynton@gmail.com | Evan Spiegel | evan.spiegal@snapchat.com | Social Media Service |
| Spotify | 150 Greenwich St 62nd Floor, New York, NY 10007 | N/A | Daniel Ek | daniel@spotify.com | Dainel Ek | daniel@spotify.com | Digital Music Service |
| Starbucks Corporation | 2401 Utah Avenue South Seattle, WA 98134 | 206-447-1575 | Howard Schultz (Matt Fitch VP) | VP's (mftch@starbucks.com) | Kevin Johnson | kjohnson@starbucks.com | Coffee Shops |
| Strava Inc. | 208 Utah St FL 2, San Francisco, CA, 94103-4871 | 415-374-7298 | Mike Gainey | N/A | Michael Horvath | michael@strava.com | Managed Application, Network Services & Media |
| Target | Target Plaza 1000 Nicollet Mall Minneapolis, MN 55403 | 612-304-6073 | Brian C. Cornell | brian.cornell@target.com | Brian C. Cornell | brian.cornell@target.com | Big Bix Retail Store |
| The National Collegiate Athletic Association | 700 W. Washington Street, P.O. Box 6222, Indianapolis, IND 46206-6222 | 317-917-6222 | N/A | N/A | Bob Vecchoine | bvecchione@nacda.com | A nonprofit organization that regulates student athletes from up to 1,268 North American institutions and conferences |
| Tik Tok | 5800 Bristol Pkwy, Los Angeles, CA 90034 | 844-523-3993 | Vanessa Pappas | vanessa.pappas@tiktok.com | Shou Zi Chew | shou@tiktok.com | Social Media Service |
| T-Mobile | 3618 Factoria Blvd SE, Bellevue, WA 98006 | 425-641-1140 | Timotheus Höttges | N/A | Mike Sievert | mike.sievert@t-mobile.com | Mobile Telecommunication Company |
| Toyota Motor Company North America | 6565 Headquarters Dr, Plano, TX 75024 | 469-292-4000 | Takeshi Uchiyamada | N/A | Akio Toyoda | akio.toyoda@toyota.co.jp | Automotive manufacturer |

| Company | Address | Phone | Name | Email | Contact | Email | Description |
|---|---|---|---|---|---|---|---|
| Twitter | 1355 Market Street, San Francisco, CA 94103 | 415-222-9670 | Omid Kordestani | omidk@twitter.com | Jack Dorsey | jack@twitter.com | Social Media |
| Tyson Foods | 2200 W Don Tyson Pkwy Springdale, AR 72762 | 479-290-4000 | John H. Tyson | tysonj@tyson,com | Dean Banks | sdeanbanks@gmail.com | Processor and marketer of chicken, beef, and pork |
| Uber | 1455 Market St #400, San Francisco, CA 94103 | 866-576-1039 | Ronald Sugar | N/A | Dara Khosrowshahi | khosrowshahid@uber.com | Drive away automobile service & local passenger transporatation |
| Under Armour Inc. | 1020 Hull St FL 3, Baltimore, MD 21230-5356 | 410-454-6428 | Kevin A Plank | kevin@johnsonandjennings.com | Patrik Frisk N/A (VP Fred Bealefelb Email) | fbealefelb@unarmour.com | Performance Clothing for Sports |
| United Airlines | 233 South Wacker Drive, Chicago, IL, 60606 | 872-825-4000 | Oscar Munoz | oscar.munoz@united.com | Scott Kirby | scott.kirby@united.com | Major American Airline |
| UPS | 55 Glenlake Parkway NE, Atlanta, GA 30328 | 800-742-5877 | David Abney | david.abney@ups.com | David Abney | david.abney@ups.com | An American multinational shipping & receiving and supply chain management company |
| Walmart | 702 SW 8TH St, Bentonville, AR, 72716-6299 | 479-273-4000 | Greg Penner | gpenner@columbiaframe.com | Doug McMillon | Doug.McMillon@wal-mart.com | Retail Store |
| Wayfair Inc. | 4 Copley Place, Floor 7, Boston, MA 02116 | 617-532-6100 | Niraj Shah | nshah@wayfair.com | Niraj Shah (Co-Chairman) | nshah@wayfair.com | Online Shopping (E-Commerce) |
| YouTube | 901 Cherry Ave. San Bruno, CA 94066 | 650-253-0000 | N/A | N/A | Susan Diane Wojcicki | susan@youtube.com | Online Video Sharing & Social Media Platform |
| Zara | Beekman Regent Condominium, 750 Lexington Ave, New York, NY 10022 | 212-355-1415 | Pablo Isla | N/A | Dilip Patel (President) | dilippa@uk.inditex.com | Apparel Company |

# American Woke Company Boycott List

| Company Name | Facebook Handle | Facebook Link | Instagram | Twitter |
|---|---|---|---|---|
| Abercrombie & Fitch, Co. | @abercrombieofficial | https://www.facebook.com/abercrombieofficial/ | @abercrombie | @Abercrombie |
| Accenture | @accenture | https://www.facebook.com/accenture/ | @accenture | @Accenture |
| Adidas | @adidas | https://www.facebook.com/adidas/ | @adidas | @adidasUS |
| Adobe Inc. | @Adobe | https://www.facebook.com/Adobe/ | @adobe | @Adobe |
| Airbnb | @airbnb | https://www.facebook.com/airbnb/ | @airbnb | @Airbnb |
| AMC Theatres | @amctheatres | https://www.facebook.com/amctheatres/ | @amctheatres | @AMCTheatres |
| Apple Inc. | @apple | https://www.facebook.com/apple/ | @apple | @Apple |
| Asurion Corporation | @Asurion | https://www.facebook.com/Asurion/ | @asurion | @Asurion |
| AT&T | @ATT | https://www.facebook.com/ATT/ | @att | @ATT |
| Bain & Company | @bainandcompany | https://www.facebook.com/bainandcompany/ | @bainandcompany | @BainandCompany |
| Bank of America | @BankofAmerica | https://www.facebook.com/BankofAmerica/ | @bankofamerica | @BankofAmerica |
| Bed, Bath & Beyond | @BedBathAndBeyond | https://www.facebook.com/BedBathAndBeyond/ | @bedbathandbeyond | @BedBathBeyond |
| Belk | @Belk | https://www.facebook.com/Belk/ | @belk | @belk |
| Ben & Jerry Ice Cream | @benandjerrysUS | https://www.facebook.com/benandjerrysUS/ | @benandjerrys | @benandjerrys |
| Best Buy | @bestbuy | https://www.facebook.com/bestbuy/ | @bestbuy | @BestBuy |
| Bing | @Bing | https://www.facebook.com/Bing/app/489347001448444/ | @bing | @bing |
| BMC Software | @bmcsoftware | https://www.facebook.com/bmcsoftware/ | @bmcsoftware | @BMCSoftware |

| Boston Consulting Group | @BostonConsultingGroup | https://www.facebook.com/BostonConsultingGroup/ | @BCG |
|---|---|---|---|
| Calvin Klein (Owned by PVH Corp.) | @CalvinKlein | https://www.facebook.com/CalvinKlein/ | @CalvinKlein |
| Capital One | @capitalone | https://www.facebook.com/capitalone/ | @CapitalOne |
| Chewy Inc. | @Chewy | https://www.facebook.com/Chewy/ | @Chewy |
| Chipotle | @chipotle | https://www.facebook.com/chipotle/ | @ChipotleTweets |
| Cisco Systems | @cisco | https://www.facebook.com/cisco/ | @Cisco |
| Citigroup | @citi | https://www.facebook.com/citi/ | @Citi |
| CNN | @cnn | https://www.facebook.com/cnn/ | @CNN |
| Coca Cola | @TheCocaColaCo | https://www.facebook.com/TheCocaColaCo/ | @CocaCola |
| Colony Brands Inc. | @ColonyBrandsInc | https://www.facebook.com/ColonyBrandsInc/ | @ColonyBrandsInc |
| Comcast Corporation | @comcast | https://www.facebook.com/comcast/ | @comcast |
| Costco | @Costco | https://www.facebook.com/Costco/ | @Costco |
| Cover Girl - Owned by Coty | @covergirl | https://www.facebook.com/covergirl/ | @COVERGIRL |
| Delta Airlines Inc. | @delta | https://www.facebook.com/delta/ | @Delta |
| Diacom Corporation | @DiacomCorporation | https://www.facebook.com/Diacom-Corporation-499585250086641/?ref=ts&fref=ts | @Diacomcorp |
| Disney | @Disney | https://www.facebook.com/Disney/ | @Disney |
| Dollar General Corporation | @dollargeneral | https://www.facebook.com/dollargeneral/ | @DollarGeneral |
| Dow Chemical Company | @dow | https://www.facebook.com/dow/ | @DowChemical |
| Estee Lauder Companies | @EsteeLauder | https://www.facebook.com/EsteeLauder/ | @EsteeLauder |

| Company | | URL | | |
|---|---|---|---|---|
| Etsy | @EtsyUSA | https://www.facebook.com/Etsy-USA-1018898016513368/ | @etsy | @Etsy |
| Expedia Group | @Expedia.ca | https://www.facebook.com/Expedia.ca/?brand_redir=6406703767 9 | @expedia | @ExpediaGroup |
| Facebook | @facebook | https://www.facebook.com/facebook/ | @facebook | @Facebook |
| Gap Inc. | @GapInc | https://www.facebook.com/GapInc/ | @gapinc | @GapInc |
| General Motors | @generalmotors | https://www.facebook.com/generalmotors/ | @generalmotors | @GM |
| Girl Scouts | @GirlScoutsUSA | https://www.facebook.com/GirlScoutsUSA/ | @girlscouts | @girlscouts |
| GoDaddy | @GoDaddy | https://www.facebook.com/GoDaddy/ | @godaddy | @GoDaddy |
| Goldman Sachs | @goldmansachs | https://www.facebook.com/goldmansachs/ | @goldmansachs | @GoldmanSachs |
| Goodyear | @goodyear.sa | https://www.facebook.com/goodyear.sa/ | @goodyear | @goodyear |
| Google | @Google | https://www.facebook.com/Google/ | @google | @Google |
| Groupon, Inc. | @Groupon | https://www.facebook.com/Groupon/ | @groupon | @Groupon |
| GrubHub | @grubhub | https://www.facebook.com/grubhub/ | | |
| Harrys, Inc. | @hapostrophe | https://www.facebook.com/hapostrophe/ | @harrys | @Harrys |
| HP | @HP | https://www.facebook.com/HP/ | @hp | @HP |
| Hyundai Motor Company USA | @Hyundai | https://www.facebook.com/Hyundai/ | @hyundaiusa | @Hyundai |
| IBM | @IBM | https://www.facebook.com/IBM/ | @ibm | @IBM |
| Ikea | @IKEAUSA | https://www.facebook.com/IKEAUSA/ | @ikeausa | @IKEAUSA |
| Instagram | @instagram | https://www.facebook.com/instagram/ | @instagram | @instagram |
| Intel | @Intel | https://www.facebook.com/Intel/ | @intel | @intel |

| Company | Handle | Facebook URL | Handle | Handle |
|---|---|---|---|---|
| JC Penney | @jcp | https://www.facebook.com/jcp/ | @jcpenney | @jcpenney |
| Jet Blue | @JetBlue | https://www.facebook.com/JetBlue/ | @jetblue | @JetBlue |
| Kohl's Corporation | @kohls | https://www.facebook.com/kohls/ | @kohls | @Kohls |
| L'oreal USA | @lorealgroupe | https://www.facebook.com/lorealgroupe/?brand_redir=268763679829571 | @lorealgroupe | @loreal |
| LinkedIn | @LinkedIn | https://www.facebook.com/LinkedIn/ | @linkedin | @LinkedIn |
| Lyft | @Lyft | https://www.facebook.com/lyft/ | @lyft | @lyft |
| Macy's | @Macys | https://www.facebook.com/Macys/ | @macys | @Macys |
| Mailchimp | @mailchimp | https://www.facebook.com/mailchimp/ | @mailchimp | @Mailchimp |
| Major League Baseball (MLB) | @mlb | https://www.facebook.com/mlb/ | @mlb | @MLB |
| Marvel | @marvelstudios | https://www.facebook.com/marvelstudios/ | @marvelstudios | @MarvelStudios |
| Mattress Firm Bedquarters | @MattressFirm | https://www.facebook.com/MattressFirm/ | @mattressfirm | @MattressFirm |
| McDonalds Corporation | @McDonalds | https://www.facebook.com/McDonalds/ | @mcdonalds | @McDonalds |
| Microsoft Corporation | @Microsoft | https://www.facebook.com/Microsoft/ | @microsoft | @Microsoft |
| Mondelez International | @mondelezinternational | https://www.facebook.com/mondelezinternational/ | @mondelez_international | @MDLZ |
| NBA | @nba | https://www.facebook.com/nba | @nba | @NBA |
| Netflix, Inc. | @netflix | https://www.facebook.com/netflix/ | @netflix | @Netflix |
| New York Times | @nytimes | https://www.facebook.com/nytimes/ | @nytimes | @nytimes |
| Nike | @nike | https://www.facebook.com/nike/ | @nike | @Nike |
| Nordstrom | @Nordstrom | https://www.facebook.com/Nordstrom/ | @nordstrom | @Nordstrom |

| Nvidia Corporation | @NVIDIA | https://www.facebook.com/NVIDIA/ | @nvidia | @nvidia |
| Office Depot | @OfficeDepot | https://www.facebook.com/OfficeDepot/ | @officedepot | @officedepot |
| P&G | @proctergamble | https://www.facebook.com/proctergamble/ | @proctergamble | @ProcterGamble |
| Pepsico, Inc. | @PepsiCo | https://www.facebook.com/PepsiCo/ | @pepsico | @PepsiCo |
| Pinterest | @pinterest | https://www.facebook.com/pinterest/ | @pinterest | @Pinterest |
| Reddit | @reddit | https://www.facebook.com/reddit/ | @reddit | @Reddit |
| Salesforce | @SalesforceCA | https://www.facebook.com/SalesforceCA/?brand_redir=459043090801393 | @salesforce | @salesforce |
| Sephora | @sephora | https://www.facebook.com/sephora | @sephora | @Sephora |
| Simon & Shuster | @Simonandschuster | https://www.facebook.com/Simonandschuster/ | @simonandschuster | @simonschuster |
| Snap Chat | @officialsnapchatapp | https://www.facebook.com/officialsnapchatapp/ | N/A | @Snapchat |
| Starbucks Corporation | @Starbucks | https://www.facebook.com/Starbucks/ | @starbucks | @Starbucks |
| Strava Inc. | @Strava | https://www.facebook.com/Strava/ | @strava | @Strava |
| T-Mobile | @TMobile | https://www.facebook.com/TMobile/ | @tmobile | @TMobile |
| Target | @target | https://www.facebook.com/target/ | @target | @Target |
| The National Collegiate Athletic Association | @ncaa1906 | https://www.facebook.com/ncaa1906/ | @ncaa | @NCAA |
| Tik Tok | @tiktok | https://www.facebook.com/tiktok/ | @tiktok | @tiktok |
| Toyota | @toyota | https://www.facebook.com/toyota/ | @toyota | @Toyota |
| Twitter | @TwitterInc | https://www.facebook.com/TwitterInc/ | @twitter | @Twitter |

| Tyson Foods | @TysonFoods | https://www.facebook.com/TysonFoods/ | @tysonfoods | @TysonFoods |
|---|---|---|---|---|
| Under Armour Inc. | @UnderArmour | https://www.facebook.com/UnderArmour/ | @underarmour | @UnderArmour |
| United Airlines | @United | https://www.facebook.com/United/ | @united | @united |
| UPS | @ups | https://www.facebook.com/ups/ | @ups | @UPS |
| Walmart | @walmart | https://www.facebook.com/walmart/ | @walmart | @Walmart |
| Wayfair Inc. | @WayfairCA | https://www.facebook.com/WayfairCA/?brand_redir=21568633178877 | @wayfair | @Wayfair |
| YouTube | @youtube | https://www.facebook.com/youtube/ | @youtube | @YouTube |
| Zara | @Zara | https://www.facebook.com/Zara/ | @zara | @ZARA |

# ABOUT THE AUTHORS

**Wayne Allyn Root** (aka WAR) is not your typical CEO. The bestselling author of 15 books—including "TRUMP RULES," "The Power of Relentless," "The Ultimate Obama Survival Guide" and "The Murder of the Middle Class" prefers the titles SOB, HEB and MR—for "Son of a Butcher" "Human Energizer Bunny" and "Mr. Relentless." The media calls him "the conservative warrior" and "the capitalist evangelist." President Trump says "Wayne knows how to win." Premier Radio Network host Bill Cunningham calls Wayne "One of the great conservative thinkers in America."

Wayne is a high-energy, dynamic, outspoken, fiery, combative, controversial, unapologetic, in-your-face, New York businessman, Las Vegas gaming CEO, reality TV show producer, and former Presidential candidate, turned conservative media superstar.

*Remind you of anyone?*

That could be why even the liberal Trump-hating "Daily Beast" called Wayne, "The Donald Trump of Las Vegas."

Wayne is best known for his relentless energy, enthusiasm and passion for America, American exceptionalism, the great American middle class, conservatism, capitalism, economic freedom, small business, and the American Dream.

This former 2008 Libertarian Vice Presidential nominee is the host of the nationally syndicated *"Wayne Allyn Root: Raw & Unscripted"* on USA Radio Network daily from 6 p.m. to 9 p.m. Eastern (3 p.m. to 6 p.m. Pacific). Former President Trump was a recent guest on Wayne's show.

Wayne was named to the *"Talkers Heavy Hundred"* list of the top 100 radio talk show hosts in America in 2019, 2020, and 2021. Wayne joins the list with the superstars of talk radio, including the late Rush Limbaugh, Sean Hannity, Dave Ramsey, Mark Levin, Michael Savage, Dan Bongino, Ben Shapiro and Glenn Beck.

Wayne's popular daily podcast is titled, *"WAR RAW."* It is available at I-Tunes, Spotify, iHeart, Apple, Amazon, Google Play, or wherever you listen to podcasts.

Wayne's latest book, *"TRUMP RULES"* is a #1 best-seller in a dozen business and political categories. It is Wayne's 14th book.

Wayne's newspaper column is read in newspapers across the USA, syndicated by *Creators Syndicate.*

Wayne is a former lead anchorman and host of five shows at *CNBC* (then known as Financial News Network).

Wayne was the opening speaker at every presidential campaign event in Las Vegas for candidate Donald J. Trump. He was personally-chosen by President Donald J. Trump as opening speaker for Trump's first Las Vegas visit as President of the United States in September 2018.

Wayne speaks to conservative and business groups and conferences across the USA on the topics of conservative politics, capitalism, economics, business leadership, entrepreneurship; and of course, the "TRUMP RULES" of winning at business, politics and life.

Wayne is a S.O.B. (son of a butcher). Wayne was born into a blue-collar Jewish family. Wayne took Jesus Christ as his savior 30 years ago. This unique religious and spiritual combination of Judaism and Christianity, and Wayne's love of Israel, led Wayne to call President Trump "the greatest President in world history for the Jewish people and Israel" on national TV—leading to a liberal media meltdown across the globe. President Trump personally tweeted his thanks to Wayne multiple times.

Wayne was honored in 2006 with a 180-pound granite star on the "Las Vegas Walk of Stars." His star sits on Las Vegas Blvd in front of the Paris Resort & Casino. Wayne joins the legends of Vegas including Elvis, Liberace, Wayne Newton, Frank Sinatra, Dean Martin, Sammy Davis Jr., Bobby Darin and Siegfried & Roy.

Wayne resides in Las Vegas, Nevada with his family.

**Nicky Billou** is an immigrant from the Middle East, and grateful for the freedoms found in the West. He is a champion for freedom, free expression, free enterprise and entrepreneurs. He is the #1 International Best Selling Author of the book: *Finish Line ThinkingTM: How to Think and Win Like a Champion*, and *The Thought Leader's Journey: A Fable of Life*. He is the host of the #1 Podcast in the world on thought leadership, "The Thought Leader Revolution"

www.TheThoughtLeaderRevolution.com. In this role, Nicky has interviewed over 300 of the world's top Thought Leaders. He is an in-demand and highly inspirational speaker to corporate audiences. He is and advisor and confidante to some of the most successful and dynamic entrepreneurs in Canada & the US.

Nicky is the co-founder of eCircle Academy (www.eCircleAcademy.com) where he runs a yearlong Mastermind & Educational program working with Coaches, Consultants, Corporate Trainers, Clinic Owners, Realtors, Mortgage Brokers and other service-based Entrepreneurs, positioning them as authorities in their niche. He is the creator of the Thought Leader/Heart Leader™ Designation.

He also writes on issues of business, culture and politics for Politicrossing, including profiles of Wayne Allyn Root, Dana White of the UFC, #1 bestselling business author Ken Blanchard, Barbara Corcoran (star of the hit series "Shark Tank"), George Ross of "The Apprentice," Jack Canfield & Mark Victor Hansen (authors of "Chicken Soup For The Soul"), Scott Adams (the creator of the "Dilbert" cartoon series), Roger Simon (Founder of PJ Media & Academy Award nominated screenwriter), skateboarding legend Tony Hawk, and Ryan Michler, host of "The Order of Man" podcast.

To contact Wayne for a speech or media appearance:

**Wayne Allyn Root**
ROOTforAmerica.com
WayneRoot@gmail.com
Wayne@WayneRoot.com

**PH:**
(888) 444-ROOT(7668)

**Address:**
1930 Village CenterCircle
Ste 3-376
Las Vegas, NV 89134

**Parler:**
@RealWayneRoot

**To contact Nicky Billou:**
Nicky@ecircle.ca

**PH:**
416-629-7481

Made in the USA
Monee, IL
03 October 2021

79282844R00075